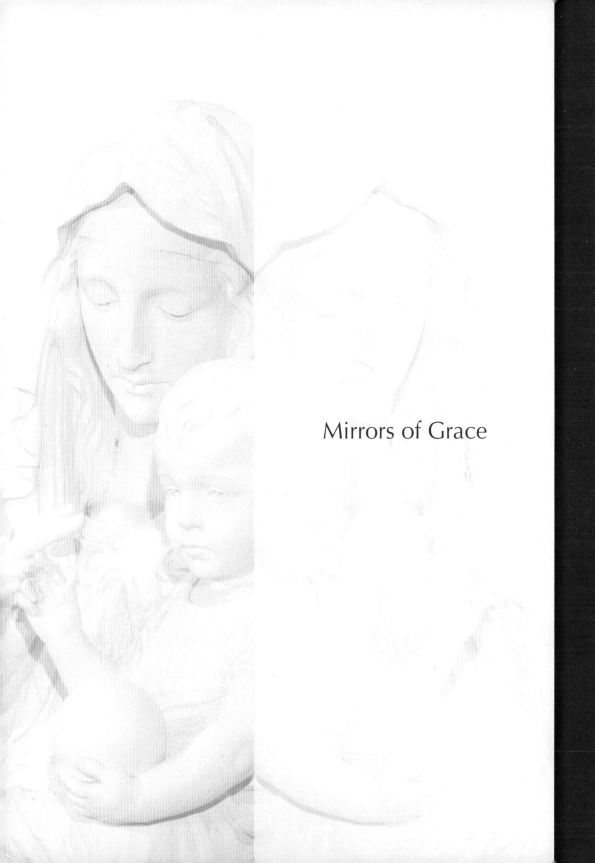

Mirrors of Grace

Mirrors of Grace

Joseph R. Veneroso, M.M.

ORBIS BOOKS
Maryknoll, New York 10545

Founded in 1970, Orbis Books endeavors to publish works that enlighten the mind, nourish the spirit, and challenge the conscience. The publishing arm of the Maryknoll Fathers and Brothers, Orbis seeks to explore the global dimensions of the Christian faith and mission, to invite dialogue with diverse cultures and religious traditions, and to serve the cause of reconciliation and peace. The books published reflect the views of their authors and do not represent the official position of the Maryknoll Society. To learn more about Maryknoll and Orbis Books, please visit our website at www.maryknollsociety.org.

Published by Orbis Books, Maryknoll, NY 10545-0302.

Manufactured in the United States of America
All photos provided courtesy of Maryknoll Mission Archives.

Library of Congress Cataloging-in-Publication Data
Veneroso, Joseph R.
Mirrors of grace : the spirit and spiritualities of the Maryknoll Fathers and Brothers / by Joseph R. Veneroso.
        p. cm.
    ISBN 978-1-57075-928-4 (cloth)
        1. Catholic Foreign Mission Society of America. I. Title.
    BV2300.C35V46 2011
    266'.2--dc22
                                                2010042948

With gratitude to Maryknoll's
countless benefactors and
supporters whose generosity
and prayers over the last
one hundred years have made
our mission work possible.

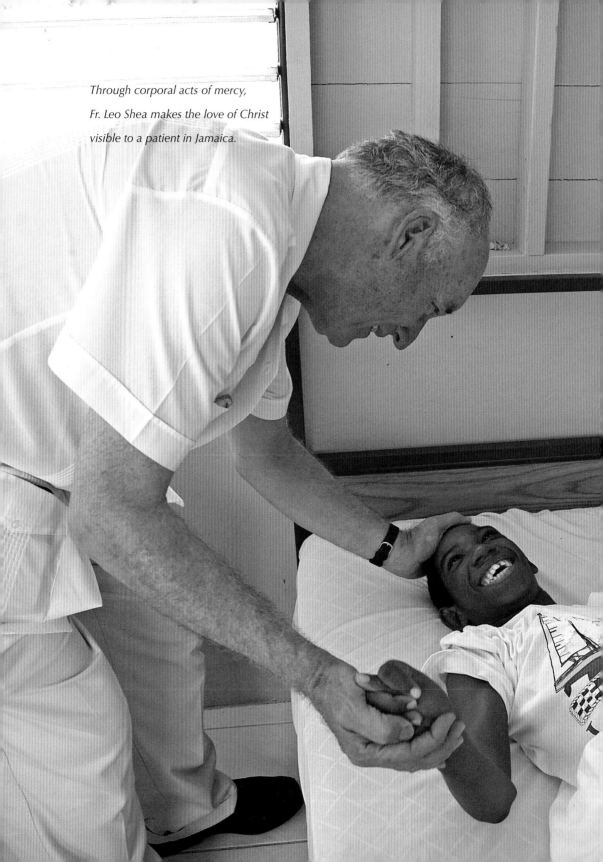

Through corporal acts of mercy, Fr. Leo Shea makes the love of Christ visible to a patient in Jamaica.

"For the reign of God is not about eating and drinking but justice and peace and joy in the Holy Spirit."

—Romans 14:17

Outward

Like mirrors, Maryknoll missioners focus outward. They reflect the holiness, goodness, beauty, and truth they see in the culture, language, and most of all, lives of people they serve in other countries. They do this to restore the divine image in which all humans are made, as well as to magnify that divine light which enlightens every man and woman in the world (John 1:9). They feel called to travel to fields afar for the love of Jesus Christ and, through a variety of works and witness, to extend the reign of God in all places among all peoples.

Yet a reflection can only be as true as the mirror. Distorted or smudged mirrors reflect poorly, if at all. Thus, from the beginning, Maryknoll's primary purpose, according to its Constitutions, has been "the personal sanctification of its members." This goes beyond acts of personal piety. It incorporates and integrates all aspects of our lifelong development as Catholic men. In recent years many Maryknollers have begun attending to their own inner work of spiritual, emotional, and psychological well-being, the better to reflect the holiness they encounter with as little distortion as possible. The more comfortable Maryknollers are in their own skins, to use a current expression, the more capable and effective they are in communicating God's call to renewal to others. Thus, in addition to the many spiritual renewal programs and updating to remain current on the latest trends in understanding our Church and world, on a personal level many missioners have benefited immensely from the various twelve-step programs, which in turn formed the basis for their spiritualities and, by extension, their ministries and lives. Like Peter who, having personally experienced his own need for forgiveness and healing, was able to feed Christ's sheep, men in recovery have proven to be effective ministers in a world badly in need of forgiveness, healing, and recovery on many levels.

Anything but passive, Maryknoll missioners are in fact two-way mirrors. What they see and experience overseas profoundly affects and changes them. People impact Maryknollers, for good or ill, as much if not more than missioners impact people. At special times some missioners may also reveal their own innermost thoughts, feelings, and personal struggles. Sharing their doubts as well as their faith breaks down the barrier between "us" and "them." For Maryknollers, all peoples are partners on this exciting journey together.

For the past one hundred years, Maryknollers have gone to Asia, Latin America, and Africa in the name of Jesus Christ, to announce, discover, and celebrate the mystery of God present among people, especially the poor. In various languages and through a multitude of works, Maryknollers tell the story of what God did in ages past and what God is doing here and now.

Preferential Option for the Poor
This raises some questions. First, why emphasize the poor?

Missioners do not hold a romanticized notion about poor people being better, holier, or more deserving than others. If they do, the poor themselves quickly disabuse them of it. Poor people can be as demanding and annoying as everyone else. Rather, following the call of Latin American bishops meeting in Medellín, Colombia, in 1968, many Maryknollers made a "preferential option for the poor." In other words, they acknowledged the biblical truth that the poor have a just and distinct claim on the spiritual and material resources of the Church. This concept, while not always explicit, has run throughout Catholic social teaching for two millennia. Indeed, concern for the *anawim*, or the "poor of God," permeates the prophetic writings of the Hebrew Scriptures. In Luke's Gospel, Jesus calls the poor blessed. In

Matthew's account of the Last Judgment, these "least of our brothers and sisters" are none other than Christ himself.

Poor people are not simply the objects of Christian charity and service. They have an active role to play in teaching the rest of the world about faith, generosity, and relying on God alone. Conversely, the preferential option for the poor certainly does not exclude working among other classes of people. On the contrary, when missioners do work with other people, especially the rich and the influential, they remain mindful of the effect their decisions, actions, and policies have on the poor. Whenever possible, missioners bring up the concerns of the poor when dealing with those in positions of power, thus giving a voice to the voiceless. What's more, to the extent they are able, Maryknollers often live among the poor, stand in solidarity with the poor, and at times even suffer the same fate as the poor.

That being said, Maryknollers are mindful they can never really be poor. Education, health care, and simply being citizens of the United States give them options and opportunities unavailable to the poor of the world. Yet the very fact that they are willing to eschew such benefits to stand in solidarity with the poor in their struggle, even for a time, has itself proven a rich, albeit silent witness to the gospel of Christ. Why an American would give up all the comforts and security of life in the United States to live and work among the poor in other countries only makes sense when answered: for the love of God.

The poor have much to teach
about depending on God.

Original Maryknoll Hymn,
by Francis X. Ford, ca. 1916

To raise up sterling men for God
Maryknoll, my Maryknoll,
Whose blood may stain the heathen sod,
Maryknoll, my Maryknoll,
This is thy aim, thy sacred call,
To bring Christ's name and grace to all
God speed thee on to save man's soul,
O House of God, my Maryknoll!

O Mary, the Apostles' Queen
For Maryknoll, thy Maryknoll
Throughout this country do thou glean
For Maryknoll, thy Maryknoll
Vocations to the darkened East
That needs the offering hand of priest
To bless it, 'ere Death sounds its toll,
From Maryknoll, thy Maryknoll.

Updated Maryknoll Hymn, revised 1990

Proclaim God's Kingdom here on earth,
Maryknoll, my Maryknoll
To lift up all to their true worth,
Maryknoll, thy Maryknoll
This is your aim, your sacred call,
To bring Christ's name and grace to all.
God speed you on, attain your goal
O House of God, my Maryknoll!

O Mary, the Apostles' Queen
For Maryknoll, your Maryknoll
Throughout this country do you glean,
For Maryknoll, your Maryknoll
Vocations to announce new life,
Assist the poor to end their strife,
To radiate God's love to all,
Through Maryknoll, your Maryknoll.

New Motivation for Mission

Another question: If God is already present among people in other lands, then why go?

Contemporary Catholic appreciation for God's presence in the world and sensitivity toward people of other religions certainly make missioners more respectful, if not more humble, in their approach to other religions and cultures. Time was when missionaries had to go and baptize as many people as possible; that was the main purpose of mission. Not anymore. Unfortunately, with this new understanding that God is already present and active among people has come a regrettable loss of any sense of urgency to mission. To rekindle that "missionary zeal," it is necessary for missioners to focus on people's needs, material as well as spiritual.

For millennia, Christian missioners pointed to the Great Commission of Mark 16:15 ("Go into the whole world and preach the good news to every creature") as their divinely mandated duty, indeed solemn obligation to travel the world and proclaim the good news. In addition to every Christian's responsibility to share his or her faith, modern missioners not only recognize their duty to spread the gospel, but also every person's right and very critical need to hear it. Even a perfunctory scanning of any day's headlines shows nothing more urgent than saving our world from its self-destructive collision course with total annihilation through unfettered greed, lust for power, overindulgence, and war. The gospel of peace, forgiveness, reconciliation, justice, and love is the only and urgent remedy, today more than ever.

Having visited one of Cambodia's killing fields where the skulls and bones of twenty thousand victims of the Pol Pot regime were displayed, Fr. John Barth naturally felt depressed, especially so because it was Christmas. Then his spirit lifted when the people of the village of Chrey Thum welcomed him with shouts of "Sua sa-die Bon Noel!" Merry Christmas! This reminded him God became one of us in a small town like Chrey Thum to free the world of war and hatred.

A long history of exploitation, poverty, and violence has robbed people of hope. Just as people cannot see their own faces unaided by a mirror, they have forgotten or are unaware of their own worth and dignity as precious children of God. It usually takes an outsider to reflect their God-given worth back to them. The Christian missioner's vocation is to tell people about the love of God for them made visible and accessible through Jesus Christ. This revelation empowers them to become subjects rather than objects of their circumstances, their history, and their future. What they do with this powerful and life-changing awareness and how they choose to respond to it is up to them.

As mentioned earlier, missioners from the most powerful country on earth willing to leave behind the comforts and amenities of life in the States to live and work among the poor overseas says more about the true nature of God's reign than do most sermons. Poor people everywhere suffer greatly from economic and political decisions beyond their control. Once they realize their worth and ability to better their situation, change happens. Indeed, it becomes inevitable. With this awareness comes conversion, liberation, and by God's grace, salvation, not only for the people but also for the missioners themselves. By helping others appreciate their own holiness and worth, the sanctification of Maryknoll's members progresses.

That is why the Holy Spirit sends missioners to the "ends of the earth," not just geographically but socially—in other words, to the very fringes of human society. Maryknollers look for sparks of the divine in the most remote, unlikely places and people: among refugee Buddhist monks fleeing persecution from Myanmar, transgendered youth facing violent persecution and death in Brazil, abandoned children and orphans of mixed race in Korea, former gang members in Honduras, or people living with and dying from AIDS in a Kenya slum. Over the course of a century Maryknoll has received abundant accolades for such corporal acts of mercy; at other times, not so much.

Just as mirrors reflect the ugly as well as the beautiful, the bad as well as the good, at times missioners shine the light of the gospel on the darker side of human existence, exposing sinful persons as well as sinful systems—worker exploitation and human trafficking, for example—that distort God's image and block God's grace. For such efforts, some Maryknollers have received public criticism, death threats, arrest, deportation, and even martyrdom. Yet this is no different from what people who struggle for justice endure every day around the world. The reign of God continues to suffer violence (Matthew 11:12).

At a gathering to honor Nobel Peace Prize–winner Archbishop Desmond Tutu, the South African prelate was introduced to some Maryknollers in the reception line. "Maryknollers!" he exclaimed. "You're all troublemakers!" Then he added with a twinkle in his eye, "Thank God!"

Fr. Joseph Veneroso holds up a mirror for a Korean man at a flea market.

Spirituality and Religion
Another question: So what exactly is spirituality?

These days there is much talk, especially among younger people, about being "spiritual, not religious." While the distinction between religion and spirituality is valid, having one without the other is incomplete. More often than not, such people who claim to be spiritual but not religious became discouraged, disillusioned, or disgusted with organized religion and the sad history—both ancient and recent—of believers falling far short of the lofty ideals they profess. Corruption, lust for power, and hypocrisy have sullied the reputation of religions. The Gospels contain ample examples of religious people in Jesus' time—the scribes, Pharisees, and Sadducees—who for all their outward religiosity lacked a sound spirituality. So we can see the pitfalls of religion without spirituality, but spirituality without religion may also prove insufficient. Religion without spirituality is lifeless; spirituality without religion is aimless. Together they are priceless.

The word "religion" comes from the Latin *religare*, "to bind fast," and by definition is concerned with rules and rituals that bind together and identify people with a shared belief; spirituality, on the other hand, is about recognizing and fostering healthy relationships between oneself and God—or a Higher Power—with others, and with all Creation. It helps us appreciate how we are connected to God, to one another, and to the Earth. Spirituality seeks out, cultivates, and celebrates these connections. At its core is a healthy and honest relationship between you and yourself. This lies at the heart of the Great Commandment, "You shall love the Lord your God with all your heart, with all your soul, with all your mind and with all your strength. . . . You shall love your neighbor as yourself" (Mark 12:30–31).

In Kigali, Rwanda, after the genocidal war between Hutu and Tutsi groups, both predominantly Catholic, a Tutsi woman was asked to identify her husband's murderer. Although she knew who it was, according to Fr. Joe Healey, she refused because the man would be arrested, imprisoned, and most likely killed in return. More widows. More orphans. More suffering. "The killing has to stop somewhere," she said. "One murder does not justify another killing. We have to break the cycle of violence and end this genocide."

The relationship between spirituality and religion, and our actions in combining the two can also be expressed through another metaphor. A sailboat needs a sail for power and movement, a keel to add stability and a rudder for direction. Without the sail (spirituality) the ship cannot catch the wind, or spirit, if you will. The ship lacks power and drifts aimlessly with any current. But without the keel (religion), the ship lacks balance and cannot remain upright. The higher one wants to reach, the deeper one must be willing to go. Religion provides depth even as spirituality gives height and inspiration.

Religion and spirituality

With no sail, the boat stalls; with no keel, it capsizes; with no rudder, it drifts. All three, then, are essential. Yet all three depend on the skill, expertise, and knowledge of the sailor whose steady hands direct the rudder and use sail and keel to greatest advantage. With Roman Catholicism as their balancing keel and through their actions on behalf of the poor, Maryknollers display a wide range of spiritualities. Each man has his own unique way of capturing the Spirit, who blows where it will (John 3:8).

Because of the highly unlikely collection of disparate individuals known as the Maryknoll Fathers and Brothers, it is difficult, if not impossible, to describe the Society as having just one spirituality. Each member's spirituality differs as much from other Maryknollers' as individual instruments in an orchestra, to use yet another metaphor. They may be loosely grouped together, like winds and strings, but some are out of tune and some members play from different sheet music altogether. The subtitle of this book thus speaks of spiritualities in the plural and in broad terms. That being said, the occasional sublime harmony produced over the years has indeed given rise to something we can identify as the Maryknoll spirit.

This book attempts to identify and celebrate this spirit as well as some of the spiritualities of the Maryknoll Fathers and Brothers, to both underscore their uniqueness as well as to establish their oneness with the greater human family. By holding up a literary mirror to these spiritual mirrors of grace, this book hopes to magnify the light, illuminate souls, and give readers a glimpse of the eternal.

"A city set on a hill cannot be hidden."
—Matthew 5:14

"As living stones you are being
built up as a spiritual house."
—1 Peter 2:5

*Maryknoll Fathers
and Brothers
headquarters*

Introduction

From afar, the headquarters of the Maryknoll Fathers and Brothers looks for all the world like the background of some Shaolin temple in a kung-fu film. Perched atop a wooded knoll dedicated to the Virgin Mary (hence the name Maryknoll) overlooking the lower Hudson Valley in Ossining, New York, the majestic sight of the upturned, hip and gable, green-tiled roof and multiple towers takes the first-time visitor's breath away. Designed by the architect brother of Maryknoll cofounder Bishop James A. Walsh, precisely to evoke images of exotic lands and whet the appetite for life abroad, it remains the biggest Oriental-style building in the Western Hemisphere. It also captures the Society's deep affection for its first mission: China.

Closer inspection reveals another paradox. While the roof is unmistakably Oriental, the arches and stonework of the walls suggest European or Latin American influence. This improbable combination of East and West should not work, but somehow does. The same holds true for the Maryknoll Society.

Quarried from the earth during the construction of the local Croton Dam at the beginning of the twentieth century, the rocks and stones in the thick walls supporting the edifice provide an apt metaphor for the individual members of the Maryknoll Fathers and Brothers. No two are alike. Each differs in size and shape. Taken separately, some are fascinating, others plain. Some are rough, others smooth. All have chips, cracks, or faults. Yet in the hands of the Master Builder, these living stones serve a common purpose by giving shape and supporting the entire structure. Love of mission is the mortar that holds them all together.

The building itself fairly shouts mission; absent an enclosed cloister area, all sides open outward to the world. It invites and welcomes people in, only to send them out again. Embedded in the flagstone of the floor of the rotunda in Maryknoll's main entrance are brass letters in relief spelling out a circular greeting: "Pax intrantibus; salus exeuntibus" (Peace to those who enter; health—or salvation—to those who leave).

The three cornerstones of the Maryknoll movement are Bishop James A. Walsh, Father Thomas Frederick Price, and Mother Mary Joseph (Molly) Rogers, foundress of the Maryknoll Sisters. Bishop Walsh's spirituality can be described as no-nonsense, both-feet-on-the-ground Roman Catholicism tempered by a generous portion of American pragmatism. Father Price exhibited an otherworldly, head-in-the-clouds, eccentric mysticism including self-flagellation as well as a spiritual marriage with St. Bernadette, complete with an inscribed wedding ring. Surviving both Walsh and Price by decades, like a widow left with many foster children, Mother Mary Joseph probably exerted the greatest, albeit more subtle influence on the earliest development of the Fathers and Brothers as she strove to keep alive the memory and spirit of the founders. She embodied steady courage, quiet wisdom, and gentle humor.

Every Maryknoll Father and Brother fits somewhere in between these three pillars of Walsh, Price, and Rogers. To varying degrees, the spiritualities of individual Maryknollers combine and reflect elements of all three founders. That being said, not everything expressed in this book applies to every member. Often it may be a goal toward which Maryknollers strive but have yet to fully attain. Nor will every member agree with everything in this book. Such is the *sui generis*, one-of-a-kind nature of each Maryknoller. Collectively, however, the experiences and reputation of the Maryknoll Fathers and Brothers give rise to a very distinct Maryknoll spirit.

As a Society of Apostolic Life, the Maryknoll Fathers and Brothers (also known as the Catholic Foreign Mission Society of America) focus primarily on their apostolate—in this case, overseas mission work. What holds this improbable collection of motley Maryknoller men together is mission. This takes precedence over community or even prayer, yet we shall see in the following pages how both prayer and community are placed in service of mission, and indeed are indispensable elements of it.

This icon of Our Lady of Maryknoll was written by noted iconographer Father William Hart McNichols to commemorate the centennial of the Maryknoll Fathers and Brothers. Images of Our Lady of Maryknoll depict the Blessed Mother holding the Child Jesus, who in turn is holding the world. Her right hand teaches him how to bless. His left foot, pointing outward, shows our Lord eager to be about his Father's business.

An icon is more than a religious picture; it is a window into the divine and portrays Christ, the Blessed Mother, or the saints in glory. It not only inspires people to pray; it participates in the prayer, acting as a visual link between heaven and earth.

Commissioned by Maryknoll Fathers Joseph Veneroso, Gerard Hammond, and J. Edward Szendrey, this icon is unique in that Jesus resembles so many of the children missioners see every day overseas.

"I say to you that you are Peter and upon this rock I will build my church; and the gates of Hell shall not prevail against it. And I will give to you the keys to the kingdom of heaven."
—Matthew 16:18–19

Chapter One

CATHOLIC
Foreign Mission
Society of America

F ounded on the feast day of Saints Peter and Paul (June 29) in 1911, Maryknoll anchored its spirituality firmly in the traditions of these two apostles. Peter and his successors in Rome provided the unshakable rock of faith that Paul, arguably the greatest marketer as well as greatest missioner in history, felt compelled to spread throughout the known world. Both gave their lives for the faith. If mission formed the foundation for Maryknoll, martyrdom provided a glorious ideal, if not goal, toward which to strive. Adventure, excitement, and sacrificing one's life for the faith attracted increasing numbers of men willing to serve the Roman Catholic Church through overseas mission work. Everything in the early decades pointed toward limitless growth, success, and influence for Maryknoll. Its mission was clear: help establish the Roman Catholic version of Christianity overseas, especially in countries where it had yet to take root and prosper, starting in the world's most populous country—China. All was going well for Maryknoll and then, in 1962, the ground beneath its feet shifted with the ecclesial equivalent of a 9.5 earthquake.

Pope John XXIII opened up windows of opportunity for the Holy Spirit.

The Spirit of Vatican II

The Second Vatican Council (1962–1965) occurred midway in Maryknoll's first one hundred years, splitting the Society's history in two at the very pinnacle of its apparent success and popularity. Today the vast majority of Society members entered before the Council and were educated in pre–Vatican II theology, ecclesiology, and spirituality. The Latin Mass, breviary, novenas, benediction, and litanies constituted the prayer life of Maryknollers as they did for the rest of the Roman Catholic Church up until that time.

Prior to those days a Jesuit priest by the name of Father Leonard Feeney articulated and popularized a strict interpretation of the Catholic teaching—*Extra ecclesiam nulla salus* (Outside the Church there is no salvation)—that is, only baptized Roman Catholics could be saved and go to heaven. This extreme position eventually landed him in hot water with the Vatican, yet many Catholics agreed with him, or at least with his premise. Such a position certainly gave impetus to Catholic missionaries to go and save as many people as possible by baptizing them into the Roman Catholic Church.

With Vatican II, however, the emphasis and interpretation shifted dramatically. The discussion focused on what exactly we mean by "Church." Was it not greater and more inclusive than membership in the Roman Catholic Church? And what of the countless millions of people, who, through no fault of their own, never heard of Jesus? Who are we to put limits on the mercy of God? Theologians began speaking of "anonymous Christians" to describe people who did not formally belong to the Roman Catholic Church or know of Christ, but whose lives reflected gospel values. Or as Jesus put it, "And other sheep I have, that are not of this fold: them also I must bring" (John 10:16).

With radical changes in the Mass, emphasis on collegiality (shared authority by local synods of bishops with the pope), and calls for positive relationships with other religions and the secular world, Vatican II presented challenges and opportunities for the Maryknoll Society as well as for the Church at large.

Sensing an inevitable, if not immediate, shift in Roman Catholic religious life of what was once thought immutable, including the discipline of mandatory celibacy for clergy, large numbers of priests and Brothers left the Society in the years immediately following the Council. Most, but certainly not all, of those who remained in Maryknoll enthusiastically embraced Vatican II reforms, seeing them as a huge boon to mission and evangelization. Blessed Pope John XXIII had thrown open the centuries-closed windows of the Church and called for *aggiornamento*, bringing the Church up to date. From a uniform and universal Rome-centered spirituality based on conviction and absolute certainty, a new groundwork was laid promoting ongoing discernment and adaptation to read the "signs of the times" (Matthew 16:3).

Visiting the Maryknoll parish in Nimuke, Sudan, Fr. Gene Toland was impressed with the tenacity and enthusiasm of an eighty-year-old grandmother enrolled in the Rite of Christian Initiation of Adults (R.C.I.A.) program. He asked what had inspired her to convert to Catholicism. The woman explained, "I heard that we get new life in baptism, and if there's anything I need, it's new life!"

With new emphasis on building up the local church and its hierarchy, individual Maryknollers started to decline opportunities to be named bishop for overseas dioceses. Now native priests could and should become bishops. Now the heretofore mysterious if not mystical Latin Mass could be understood and celebrated in Kiswahili, Cebuano, Quechua, Cantonese, Spanish, or whatever language people spoke. Now the laity could assume their rightful identity and take an active role in liturgy, like they do in life, as the people of God. Now missioners could dialogue as peers with Orthodox Christians, Protestants, Jews, Muslims, Hindus, Buddhists, and even animists, supported by the official teaching of the Catholic Church, which "rejects nothing which is true and holy in these religions" (from the Vatican II document *Nostra Aetate*).

However, as was mentioned earlier, with this new respect for other religions and awareness of God's presence among people came a loss of that sense of urgency, which had once inspired wave upon wave of missionaries in ages past. "Saving souls" gave way to liberating the entire person from all forms of oppression—political, economic, and social, no less than spiritual. Recording baptisms into the Roman Catholic Church, referred to by some as the "numbers game," ceased to be the top priority and primary motivation for mission. Simply getting people to convert to Roman Catholicism no longer sufficed. Surely such changes were as responsible for the loss of Maryknoll members as was celibacy.

Emphasis on Human Rights and Liberation

In the post–Vatican II decades of the 1970s and 1980s, dictatorships and human rights abuses in the predominantly Catholic Philippines and many countries throughout Central and South America underscored the need for a more radical change of heart rather than a simple change of religion. How could countries, Catholic for centuries, foster such brutality? The 1971 Synod of Bishops set the tone by which Maryknoll and other mission societies would address injustice in the world: "Action on behalf of justice and participation in the transformation of the world fully appear to us as a constitutive dimension of the preaching of the Gospel, or, in other words, of the Church's mission for the redemption of the human race and its liberation from every oppressive situation." With this came the realization that "Seek first the reign of God" (episcopal motto of Bishop James A. Walsh based on Matthew 6:33) meant much more than simply spreading Catholicism. Maryknollers recognized the reign of God as something far greater and more dynamic than membership in the Roman Catholic Church.

Out of the Latin American experience and history of poverty, violence, and oppression arose a natural outgrowth of the emergence of the role of the laity and Bible study in the form of liberation theology. Articulated by Peruvian theologian Father Gustavo Gutiérrez, this seminal work was translated from Spanish and published by Orbis Books, Maryknoll's publishing house. This radical, some would say revolutionary and volatile combination of biblical reflection on one's situation along with Marxist social analysis proved highly controversial and divisive, no less among Maryknoll Society members than among prelates at the Vatican, including Pope John Paul II himself. Marxist elements notwithstanding, some would argue the most disturbing and dangerous aspect of liberation theology was not just the perceived instigation of class warfare but rather the critiquing of all institutions—economic, political, social, and even religious—including the Roman Catholic Church itself.

History has repeatedly shown the Church to be in need of ongoing conversion and reform. Yet except for the Second Vatican Council, which was truly a conversion emanating from within the very heart of the Church, institutions and men in positions of power—political or ecclesial—vehemently resist voluntary change. Eventually conditions create a climate of crisis, confronting them with the choice: reform or collapse.

While many other local theologies sprang from churches in Africa and Asia since the close of the Council, none continues to make waves as much as the theology of liberation. Despite its evolution over the decades to include a more active role for faith and prayer, liberation theology still provokes detractors to denounce and discredit Maryknoll's work among the poor, especially in Latin America, not to mention to criticize Maryknoll's public opposition to certain U.S. foreign policies and practices.

At an all-too-common roadblock and military checkpoint in El Salvador during the murderous 1980s, a Maryknoller sweated it out as a young, trigger-happy soldier barked orders for him to get out of his jeep and produce a driver's license, passport, or other form of identification. The soldier slowly scrutinized the missioner's papers, then stared at the nervous American, then looked back at the papers. The priest's fears were hardly assuaged when he noticed the soldier holding the documents upside down.

Identity Crisis

The elevation of the role of the laity precipitated an identity crisis among Maryknoll priests and Brothers. To some, the now-popular Vatican II phrase "priesthood of all the faithful" (1 Peter 2:9) meant ordained celibate priests had become redundant, or worse, obsolete. Others felt this was a much-needed and long-overdue correction to elite clericalism and privilege among clergy. The role of the lay Brother, long and perhaps still misunderstood, seemed even further diminished.

In the decades following the Second Vatican Council, the dramatic drop in the number of men entering, as well as the increase in numbers of those leaving the Society or dying, forced Maryknollers to spend considerable time rethinking and redefining their roles and identities. This uncomfortable self-reflection has provided a potentially fruitful opportunity for acceptance of vulnerability, limitations, and indeed, diminishment as a wellspring of spirituality and holiness that earlier times of abundance and expansion had disguised.

Other Vatican II changes, while more external—and one may argue, more superficial—may have contributed to the loss of vocations if not identity. Almost overnight the Maryknoll cassock disappeared, as did the cincture embroidered with the distinctive Maryknoll symbol: a red, circled "Chi Rho" symbolizing Christ in the world. To be sure, a few stalwarts continued wearing these, but for the most part post–Vatican II Maryknollers eschewed distinguishing clerical garb and became more casual, informal—if not altogether sloppy—in everyday clothing. There were many reasons for this change. In parts of Asia, missioners avoid wearing clerical collars because these are seen as visible proof that Christianity is something foreign imported from the West. In Latin America, a Roman collar may be identified with the ruling elite. In Africa, it's just too hot to wear most of the time. And in the United States, where formal clerical dress is staging a comeback, you'll find some Maryknollers who wear the Roman collar and those who don't, depending on the situation. Ideally their actions and attitudes in relating to others is all the identification they need. "By this shall all know you are my disciples, that you have love for one another" (John 13:35).

These days, seeing a large group of Maryknoll priests in black suits and Roman collars more times than not means one thing: a funeral. At Mary Queen of Apostles Chapel in the Maryknoll Center in Ossining, New York, pews with kneelers were discarded in the 1970s to allow for a return to the more ancient prayer position of standing during the canon of the Mass. Alas, forty years later this now runs counter to the re-instated practice prevalent in most U.S. dioceses of kneeling during Mass. Overseas, of course, missioners usually adopted the religious practices of the local church.

Sometimes, for lack of sufficient catechesis and preparation, a clash between Catholic cultures occurred, especially in Latin America, which had been nominally Catholic for five hundred years. In the heady days following the Council, more than one overzealous missioner incurred the wrath of irate parishioners for attempting to purge the local parish church of the crowded pantheon of statues. Not a good idea, as they were to find out. Emotions often ran higher over this than over relocating the tabernacle to a side altar for adoration. Most times, the parishioners won. Priesthood of the laity, indeed.

Controversial Vatican pronouncements on church and social issues, such as condemning artificial birth control, banning of women priests, and labeling homosexuality as intrinsically evil, found both supporters and dissenters among the Maryknoll members, as much as did other Vatican documents denouncing nuclear arms, capital punishment, free-market capitalism, and war. In all these, Maryknollers mirrored the wider divisions and dissensions spreading among the people of God, especially in the United States.

Fading Spirit of Vatican II

In recent years much of the hope and enthusiasm that Vatican II originally generated has given way to frustration, discouragement, and resignation by some in Maryknoll and the Church. They contend that many of the accomplishments and directions of the Council have been intentionally watered down, negated, or overturned. Some new Vatican directives seem outright baffling. Lay ministers of the Eucharist, for example, are still worthy to distribute the Body and Blood of Christ, but apparently not to clean the sacred vessels. The door to discussion of women's ordinations has been slammed shut, if not permanently sealed. Inclusive language in the English lectionary has been officially rejected. In the United States, a new English translation closer to the Latin Mass has been approved for use, which backpedals from the spirit of Vatican II that sought to make the liturgy more understandable and accessible by ordinary people. Recentralization of Church authority back in Rome effectively undermines the autonomy of local synods of bishops, some of whom have publicly expressed dismay at finding their agendas—and conclusions—preset by Rome. Fundamentalist tendencies have crept into Catholic Bible studies touting literal interpretations of Scripture unsupported by reputable Catholic scholars.

To be sure, some Maryknollers look at all these same developments in a positive light. They see recent pronouncements and trends as reasserting papal authority and clarifying the Church's central message and identity, which, they maintain, got muddled or misunderstood after the Council.

Trying at the same time to remain true both to the gospel and to the spirit of Vatican II, Maryknoll finds itself increasingly out of step, if not at odds, with the official Roman Catholic Church, at least as portrayed by some more conservative dioceses in the United States. Providentially, having long prided itself in working with people on the margins of society—the poor, the oppressed, the disenfranchised, the weak—Maryknoll now finds itself at the margins, but therefore even better positioned and qualified to minister to those alienated at the fringes not just of society but of the Church. Maryknoll has always done its best mission work at the margins.

Catholic Roots and Branches

For all this, Maryknollers remain deeply rooted in the liturgical traditions of Roman Catholicism, but they are more likely to practice these overseas than at home. At Maryknoll, New York, for example, the evening Angelus is still rung daily at 6 p.m., but no one stops to recite it. A faithful remnant may attend First Friday holy hour or weekly rosary. More popular are the Stations of the Cross during the Fridays of Lent where traditional and contemporary versions alternate: one week the familiar meditations of St. Alphonsus Liguori; another week the Scripture-based prayers of Pope John Paul II, or even Maryknoll's own Way of the Cross, which links the sufferings of Christ to the sufferings of people today around the world. Abroad, however, depending on the country, the Angelus, fiestas for patron saints, Corpus Christi processions, or Legions of Mary continue to mark the life of a Maryknoll missioner as they do the people. An image of the Holy Spirit in the form of a dove adorns each Maryknoll chapel, whether in the United States or overseas, as directed by Bishop Francis X. Ford, who was martyred in China and whose cause for canonization is sponsored by his home diocese of Brooklyn, New York. Since Vatican II, newer practices and devotions flourish. These include Bible study, Small (or Basic) Christian Communities, Charismatic Renewal, and Marriage Encounter, to name a few.

Patron Saints and Modern Martyrs

Maryknoll's many patron saints reflect its mission charism and spirituality. Heading that list are Ss. Peter and Paul. Besides sharing their feast day of June 29 with Maryknoll's Foundation Day, they combine the "rock" of faith with the zeal of the Apostle to the Gentiles. After Foundation Day, the biggest celebration of a patron saint is for St. Patrick (March 17), who converted Ireland and who is also the patron saint of the archdiocese of New York, in which Maryknoll headquar-

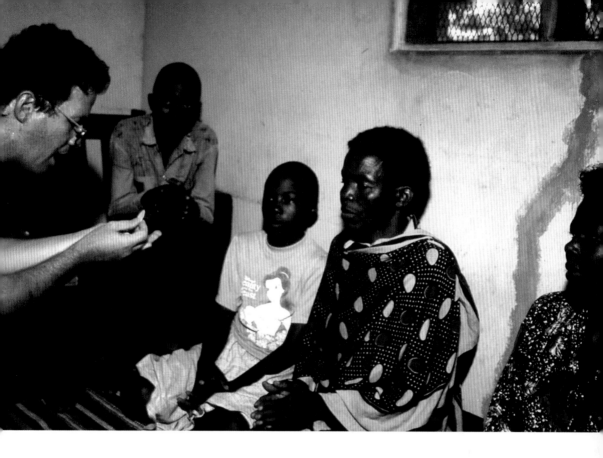

Fr. John Waldrep brings communion to a sick woman in Tanzania.

ters are located. Pope St. Pius X (September 3) not only gave permission to Fathers Walsh and Price to found a seminary to recruit and train men for mission but his singular devotion to our Blessed Mother surely also influenced the fledgling Maryknoll Society. St. Michael the Archangel (September 29) is the special patron of the Auxiliary Brothers of St. Michael, that is, the Maryknoll Brothers. St. Therese of Lisieux (October 1), the "Little Flower," though a cloistered Carmelite contemplative, reached millions through her writings. St. Teresa of Avila (October 15), Doctor of the Church, founded the Discalced Carmelites despite threats from the Inquisition. St. Francis Xavier (December 4), patron of all foreign missions, brought the faith to India and the Far East. St. Theophane Venard (also December 4) was a missioner and martyr in Vietnam. St. Boniface (June 5) spread the faith to the Germanic tribes. Although not a Maryknoll patron saint, St. Bernadette Soubirous (April 16), who received the apparitions of our Lady of Lourdes, held a special place in the heart of Father Price. Indeed, as all Maryknollers know, such was Father Price's devotion to St. Bernadette that he willed his heart be placed at the foot of her tomb in Navarre, France, where it is today.

Many recent martyrs and holy men and women inspire missioners today. These include Archbishop Oscar Romero, who was murdered in 1980 while saying Mass in El Salvador. That same year Maryknoll Sisters Maura Clarke and Ita Ford, as well as Ursuline Sister Dorothy Kazel and lay missioner Jean Donovan, suffered the same fate as the poor they served. Mohawk Indian maiden Kateri Tekakwitha further sanctified North American soil with her sufferings following the martyrdom of Jesuit missionary St. Isaac Jogues and his companions. Dominican missionary Father Bartolomé de las Casas spoke out forcefully on behalf of the oppressed Native Americans and African slaves in the sixteenth century. In the twentieth century, Dorothy Day focused attention on the plight of workers in the United States through civil disobedience and arrest. Franz Jägerstätter found in the Catholic faith grounds for conscientious objection to war and was executed by the Nazis for refusing to serve in the German Army. Last and most recently, Sister Dorothy Stang, SNDdeN, was shot to death for protecting the peoples and the rainforest of Brazil.

Father (later Bishop) Patrick Byrne spent World War II under house arrest in Kyoto, Japan. U.S. authorities feared mass suicides during the Japanese surrender. Father Pat agreed to write an editorial to assure the Japanese that American soldiers would be under strict discipline. Via radio broadcast, he also addressed the U.S. troops: "Violent, immoral, unjust, criminal behavior will not only disgrace you personally but will also disgrace your homeland. However, try to understand the suffering of the Japanese people. Put yourself in their place. Just imagine if the Nazis had been victorious and America were ravaged by atomic bombs. Please remember that this country has suffered terrible calamities, while in America not one house was destroyed." The plan succeeded.

The portraits of nine Maryknoll martyrs line one side of the main corridor at Maryknoll, New York. First was Father Gerry Donovan, killed by bandits in Manchuria in 1937. Father Robert Cairnes was reportedly murdered by Japanese troops after being forcibly removed from Sanchen Island in 1941. Father William Cummings died aboard a prisoner-of-war ship and was buried at sea in 1945. Father Otto Rauschenbach was killed by bandits in China on his way to a mission station, also in 1945. Bishop Patrick Byrne died on the infamous Death March to North Korea, having been taken prisoner in 1950 in Seoul at the onset of the Korean War. Bishop Francis Ford died in a Chinese Communist prison in 1952. Father William Kruegler was shot to death in Bolivia in 1962 by a man who became irate when the Maryknoller tried to prevent him from selling alcohol to minors. Father Vincent Capodanno was shot and killed in Vietnam in 1967 as he administered the last rites to a dying soldier. Finally, Father William Woods died in a mysterious plane crash in Guatemala in 1976 following death threats for his work on behalf of the persecuted indigenous population there.

Maryknollers being Maryknollers, many men also look for inspiration beyond the confines of the Roman Catholic Church. Missioners see Mohandas Gandhi, Albert Schweitzer, Dietrich Bonhoeffer, and Martin Luther King, Jr., as living out gospel values in their lives, though none was Catholic. This "cloud of witnesses" forms a backdrop to many missioners' spiritualities and inspires many Maryknoll ministries throughout the world.

The Blessed Virgin Mary

Marian devotions retain a special place in the hearts of Maryknollers, at home and overseas, as might be expected from a Society dedicated to the Mother of God. Many Maryknollers at the Center gather every Monday evening around the Founders' Tomb, beneath the main altar, to recite the rosary for an increase in vocations to Maryknoll.

The "mission rosary," first introduced by Bishop Fulton Sheen in the 1950s, combines a traditional devotion with a contemporary mission thrust. The first mission mystery contemplates the visit of the Magi; the second, Jesus sends out his disciples; the third, Jesus cures the centurion's servant; the fourth, Jesus talks with the Samaritan woman; and the fifth mission mystery, the conversion of St. Paul. Discovering the mission component in familiar religious practices marks just one aspect of the Maryknoll spirit.

After a hiatus of several decades, an annual May crowning once again takes place at Maryknoll, New York, and around the Maryknoll world. Likewise in preparation for the celebration of Maryknoll's one hundredth anniversary, missioners have once again begun reciting the Angelus, supreme Marian prayer of the Incarnation, prior to celebrating the Eucharist. Mary's Magnificat (Luke 1:46–55) resonates with Maryknollers who see in her prayer of praise God's own radical, preferential option for the poor. Rather than the beautiful yet passive image usually portrayed in the West, the Mary of the Magnificat glows with the fire of God's love for justice. In various ways Mary thus inspires Maryknollers throughout their mission careers. Indeed, the last official tribute paid to a deceased Maryknoller at the graveside service is the communal chanting of the Salve Regina.

"There is neither Jew nor Greek, slave nor free,
male nor female, for you are all one in Christ Jesus."
—Galatians 3:28

Chapter Two

Catholic FOREIGN Mission Society of America

L ike Ss. Peter and Paul, who argued openly as to whether Gentiles needed first to become Jews before becoming Christian (Galatians 2:1–21), Fathers James A. Walsh and Thomas F. Price disagreed strongly as to whether the new mission Society should focus its efforts exclusively overseas or include home missions in the United States. Although ultimately Walsh (and St. Paul) prevailed, ironically it was Father Price, the advocate for home mission, who went overseas with the first group in 1918 and died in Hong Kong the following year. Bishop Walsh, who saw Maryknoll exclusively as a foreign mission society, lived his entire mission life in the States and died here in 1936. This refusal by Maryknoll to include home mission in the United States as part of its vision prompted Father William Howard Bishop to found the Glenmary Fathers, Brothers, and Sisters in 1939. For his part, Walsh had set the future course: Maryknollers would work abroad.

Crossing Borders for Christ

Missioners still cross borders for Christ's sake. Unlike Peace Corps volunteers, tourists, businesspeople, or the military, Maryknollers are motivated primarily by the love of God and go overseas for the express purpose of helping people in other lands realize God also loves them. Still, this is by no means easy. For the first-time missioner, leaving family, friends, and all that is familiar to go overseas can be a wrenching and uprooting experience. Yet, providentially, this awkward and uncomfortable feeling of helplessness and vulnerability, albeit frustrating, provides the most fertile ground from which to proclaim the gospel with the greatest clarity and authenticity. As one former superior general dramatically put it, "You cannot preach the gospel effectively unless your listeners have the power to kill you."

As they have done since the time of St. Paul and the apostles, missioners live, minister, and work in foreign countries and among people other than their own. Paradoxically, while a Maryknoller lives as a stranger among strangers in a strange land, one goal of his going is to demonstrate that in Christ there is no longer a division between "us" and "them."

Foreigners become friends; friends become brothers and sisters. Missioners seek to break down the barriers separating peoples, and in so doing, build up the reign of God.

Taking a thirteen-hour mule ride through the mountainous jungle of Guatemala, Fr. Dan Jensen and his catechist had hoped to get to an out-station chapel in time for midnight Mass. Suddenly a tremendous earthquake and landslide blocked their path. Shaken but unharmed, they wondered what to do as darkness set in. They recalled a small house they'd passed a half hour earlier, so they backtracked to find a poor couple living there with their two small children about to sit down for supper. The couple gladly shared their meal with these unexpected guests: two hard-boiled eggs. It was the best feast Fr. Dan had ever tasted.

Usually the first order of business for any missioner arriving in a new land, after finding a place to live, is learning the new language. Walsh, Price, and Rogers were initially journalists and communicators, working for Catholic publications to promote interest in and support for mission work. Along with their mission cross, the earliest Maryknollers went overseas equipped with a Brownie box camera, the better to inform and inspire people back in the States about Maryknoll's mission efforts.

Maryknoll continues to place prime importance on communicating the good news in words and symbols familiar to the people. In their day, Maryknoll established notable language schools in Musoma, Tanzania; Seoul, Korea; Tai Chung, Taipei; and Davao City, the Philippines. The Maryknoll language school in Cochabamba, Bolivia, offering courses in Aymara and Quechua in addition to Spanish, continues to attract language students, Protestants as well as Catholics, from other mission-sending congregations and organizations.

Inculturation

For centuries, intentionally or not, European and American missionaries imposed their cultural values upon their unwitting hosts. Thus, the old mission churches in Hawaii look suspiciously like country parishes in New England. The first red brick cathedrals in Korea seem transplanted from France. But by using native styles of art and architecture long before the word "inculturation" was ever coined, Maryknollers wanted to honor the sense of holiness already present in the culture. Perhaps anticipating the style of their headquarters in New York, the earliest Maryknoll churches built in northern Korea and southern China during the 1920s incorporated the traditional turned-up tile roofs of Oriental buildings.

To be sure, such efforts were not always understood, much less appreciated by people in the host country. In Japan, for example, similar attempts to use Japanese styles and materials in churches met with contempt from Protestants who thought rice-paper windows, candles, and incense smacked too much of pagan worship—that is, Buddhism. Conversely in Thailand, a Buddhist country, irate Buddhists accused Christians of trying to deceive the people because some Catholic churches built in the 1970s were externally indistinguishable from Buddhist temples. With patience and perseverance, however, such misunderstandings usually were worked out over time and gave way to mutual respect, when the reverential attitude of Maryknollers toward other religions made friends, if not necessarily converts, among the people. Today, in a Buddhist temple somewhere in a remote corner of northern Thailand, a Maryknoll Brother exemplifies the Maryknoll spirit as he meditates in silence alongside his Buddhist colleagues, each respectful of the other's faith, each bowing in humble silence before the divine mystery.

A group of refugee Buddhist monks from Myanmar (Burma) peacefully protested across the street from U.N. headquarters in New York City. They carried signs denouncing the brutal crackdown on religious freedom and arrest of pro-democracy advocates by the repressive military junta in their homeland. Among the many sympathizers, supporters, and onlookers were some missioners wearing polo shirts bearing the Maryknoll logo. Seeing this, the monks excitedly said, "Maryknoll! Do you know Br. John Beeching?" The surprised missioners said they did, indeed, know Br. John, but they wondered how the monks knew him. "He taught us English in Thailand!" they said proudly.

But inculturation means much more than designing churches in local styles or dressing up the Madonna and Child in a Chinese gown, an African kanga, or a Mexican serape. The Maryknoll spirit impels missioners to look deeply into local customs and practices and uncover different ways to make visible and tangible God's love, action, and presence among the people. For example, family or communal meals form a central component of almost every society—except for twenty-first-century America, where food-on-the-run and conflicting schedules have virtually wiped out the once time-honored practice of the family gathered around a table for a meal. Breaking bread together, or sharing rice in Asia or ugali in Africa, not only expresses hospitality and fellowship, it provides a natural link between local, everyday customs and the Eucharist. The Maryknoll spirit inspires missioners, as foreigners and outsiders, to affirm local customs, foods, and traditions wherever possible.

"Can you eat kimchi?" is a Korean's way of asking, "Can you live among us as one of us?" People in each culture ask this question in one form or another to a missioner. He answers by living his life among them, with them, and for them.

A packed crowd blocked a doorway Fr. Bob McCahill needed to use on a street in Bangladesh. They were apparently listening to someone playing a flute. Squeezing his way apologetically through the tight circle of spectators, the priest suddenly came face-to-face not just with the flautist but also with a swaying, six-foot cobra. His departure was so abrupt he failed to beg their pardon.

  MIRRORS OF GRACE

On the other hand, some Western practices and symbols are meaningless to people of other cultures. An altar may represent the table of the Eucharistic banquet to Westerners, but to the people of Irian Jaya, Indonesia, for example, who do not use tables when they eat, altars mean nothing. Rather, since each family, tribe, or clan gathers around a communal fire pit for a meal, instead of side altars, smaller fire pits for different clans line the sides of the church with one main fire pit in the front where the priest presides at the Eucharist. Missioners seek ways to translate the message of Jesus not only through language but more often through actions the people understand.

Gospel as Countercultural

Sometimes, however, there may be irreconcilable differences between gospel values and deeply ingrained social practices. As one Maryknoller put it, "No culture is immaculately conceived." This may take years, if not centuries, to resolve, such as with the institution of slavery in America followed by decades of legal as well as cultural segregation. Missioners, indeed all Christians, believe the gospel must ultimately prevail in these circumstances. If, in the name of inculturation, Catholic parishes in India embraced the caste system without question and continued to treat groups of people as "untouchable," this would betray one of the core teachings of Christ. Similarly, some time ago in the southern United States, certain white parishioners refused Holy Com-

*Fr. Walt Maxcy
enjoys a Filipino feast.*

munion from an African American priest. Thanks to the stern response of the local bishop, such blasphemy did not stand. He imposed an interdict on that parish, closing its doors until the people could demonstrate true Christian community and fellowship. But as we have seen in the sixty years since the civil rights movement began in the United States, it's easier to legislate against certain acts than it is to change people's attitudes. While the United States now outlaws slavery and segregation, in pockets of American society racial prejudice and discrimination still betray both the gospel and the U.S. Constitution.

Despite laws to the contrary, gender bias has also proven particularly difficult to eradicate. Much domestic violence against women can be traced to cultures of machismo, where insecure men exaggerate presumed masculine traits to impress other men, and at the same time attract and dominate women. Precisely because they are men, Maryknoll Fathers and Brothers are in a position to effectively counter the macho mentality by treating women with respect—that is, as equals. They can actively seek out and listen to women's opinions and speak out from the pulpit against domestic violence. They can advocate for and support women in positions of authority. Maryknoll Missioners refuse to accept the unacceptable that seeks justification of oppressive policies by saying, "That's the way we've always done things around here." Of course, such a pro-women's equality stance, however halting, does not endear Maryknoll to some in secular society, let alone in the Church. On the other hand, more can certainly be done.

Cultural attitudes discriminating against blind, deaf, mentally challenged, or other people with visible disabilities are also deeply ingrained in many cultures. Some people believe persons with handicaps reflect poorly on the family, not to mention being an economic drain on their finances. In many countries the handicapped are shunted aside and kept out of sight. Eastern peoples may see persons with illnesses or disabilities as proof of the immutable law of karma, where misfortunes come as the "natural" consequences of sin in this or a previous life. Worse, such stigmas may even attach to those who interfere by trying to help.

Fr. Walter Winrich always enjoyed celebrating Mass in a far-off jungle village in Campeche, Mexico. He particularly liked talking with an old, blind Mayan gentleman who was always present at Mass. But one day when Fr. Walter arrived for a night Mass, he was concerned when his blind friend was nowhere to be seen. "Is he sick?" he asked the man's friend. "Oh no, Father," the man hastened to reassure him. "He couldn't come out because it's too dark."

Around the world one still finds pockets of prejudice against people with handicaps. Some people strongly suspect evil spirits or witchcraft at work when they see someone with a debilitating illness. Others may regard afflictions as the result of specific curses, especially the "evil eye," if not the devil. Once again, the missioner, imitating the example of Jesus who "became a curse for us" (Galatians 3:13) sees in

these "least of brethren" none other than Christ himself. In Mark 1:41, Jesus violates both social custom and the Torah by deliberately touching a man with leprosy in order to heal him. He scandalized his disciples by talking publicly to the Samaritan woman (John 4:27). He openly ate with sinners and outcasts (Luke 5:30). When Jesus declared, "The Sabbath was made for people, people were not made for the Sabbath" (Mark 2:27), he put people first, something Maryknoll still strives to do, yet not always with consistency or success.

Slowly over time, thanks in no small part to the pioneering work by Maryknollers, people's attitudes toward those with handicaps and illnesses are gradually changing.

Fr. Jim Madden and a Peruvian holy man lead the community in prayer.

As Maryknollers and others have learned from their experiences working with the sick and disabled, people with physical or emotional handicaps are no longer simply the objects of Christian charity, but more often they become conveyers of the good news to others.

Straddling two or more cultures, missioners are not just bridge builders; they are also the bridges themselves. Just as they are two-way mirrors, Maryknollers are two-way bridges, allowing culture and ideas to flow from the United States to the missions and back again, each enriching and challenging the other but always with gospel values as gatekeeper and goal. Having a foot in two different cultures sometimes means a missioner may feel either completely at home or totally out of place.

Reverse Mission

"Reverse mission," a term much in circulation in recent years, refers to what happens when missioners return home to share their experiences and insights gleaned from the lives and faith of peoples overseas. In this way, people in mission lands indirectly evangelize people back in the United States. Reverse mission also takes place among different groups within the same country. Women have much to teach men. Hispanics have much to share with Anglo Americans. Asians and African Americans can learn from each other. Of course, everyone, Maryknollers included, have personal prejudices to overcome, even though one characteristic of a missioner is to have an intellectual curiosity about and attraction to something precisely because it seems "foreign." Others may reject something outright on the same grounds since it originates with "those people." In ways both subtle and obvious, the gospel repeatedly warns against being too closed in on one's own way of thinking and doing things. The gospel challenges us to be open to the outsider who might communicate the good news to us and lead us to Christ and to salvation.

Br. John Blazo thought the youngsters at a parish in Nicaragua would enjoy a relay race in the churchyard. At his signal, the race began, but to his surprise the lead runners would periodically slow down to let their friends catch up so they could jog side by side. They instinctively replaced competition with collaboration.

We see this in Matthew's story of the Magi, foreign "pagans" who nevertheless find the Christ Child while the priests and leaders—that is, practitioners of the "right" religion—of Jerusalem did not. We hear it in Nathaniel's initial dismissal of Jesus' hometown: "Can anything good come from Nazareth?" (John 1:46). Even Jesus himself displayed cultural bias when he at first ignored the plea of the Canaanite woman on behalf of her sick daughter, calling her, in effect, a dog (Matthew 15:26). Yet her faith and persistence won him over. Maryknollers try to model their response to people after that of Jesus, who allowed a foreign woman to expand his vision and message. More controversial, Jesus held up the faith of a Roman centurion (read: foreigner, pagan, oppressor) as greater than any he had seen in all of Israel (Luke 7:9).

In recent decades, with more and more Maryknollers returning for stateside service or entering active retirement, missioners had to rethink their job description. Eventually they realized that mission work does not end just because one is back in one's own country. Nor does a missioner's concern for people stop just because he or they now live in the United States. These days, missioners understand that not all borders are national, political, or geographical. Some barriers are based on gender, race, ethnicity, social status, sexual orientation, religion, or economy. With hearts always yearning for fields afar, Maryknollers in the States continue crossing cultural borders, ministering among the new waves of immigrants: Hispanic, Vietnamese, Korean, Chinese, Filipino, and Haitian. Missioners may also act as a bridge between generations, explaining inscrutable American ways to parents and "old country" attitudes to the youngsters.

Occasionally with reverse mission also comes reverse culture shock. For missioners, coming back home can prove even more disruptive and wrenching than going abroad in the first place. Having lived years if not decades abroad, Maryknollers return to the States only to discover that they feel like strangers in their own homeland, like the proverbial fish out of water. Values have changed. People act differently. Attitudes no longer resemble those prevalent when they first went abroad. What's more, English—especially as spoken by the younger generation—suddenly sounds like a foreign language. In ministering among youth in this country, Maryknollers face the challenge of learning a "new" language just as they did when they first went overseas. In addition, the entire communication landscape has changed, with the Internet, emails, texting, and social networking forcing Maryknollers not only to learn new technology but a whole new way of communicating if they wish to get the gospel out to a new generation. As always, the mission mentality impels Maryknollers to listen and learn from the "other," even when the "foreigner" is a fellow American.

"Go therefore and make disciples of all nations,
baptizing them in the name of the Father,
and of the Son and of the Holy Spirit."
—Matthew 28:19

Chapter Three

Catholic Foreign MISSION Society of America

I n his encyclical *Redemptoris Missio* (On the Mission of the Redeemer), Blessed John Paul II identified five elements of mission: liturgy, proclamation, witness, interreligious dialogue, and human development. These are closely connected. The Eucharist impels Catholics to go out and proclaim the Gospel through word and deed, often working with men and women of other faiths to help all people, especially the poor, attain their fullest potential. To varying degrees and depending on the country and circumstances, Maryknollers incorporate each of these elements in their lives and ministries. Together with the Gospel, these form the foundation and blueprint for building the Kingdom of God.

Liturgy

How people worship reflects the degree to which they have integrated their beliefs into their lives. *Lex orandi, lex credendi, lex vivendi* is an ancient Latin maxim that means "As we pray, so we believe, and as we believe, so we live." To be sure, after Vatican II the Universal Church lost a strong, visible sign of unity when celebrating Eucharist in the vernacular replaced the traditional Latin Mass. Back in the "old days" (pre-1965), Catholics around the world felt equally united yet paradoxically excluded when the Latin Mass was celebrated in the exact same way in Belgium, Brazil, or Bangladesh. On the other hand, having a priest celebrate Mass facing the people and praying together with them instead of saying a Mass for them and with his back to them (ostensibly facing the tabernacle—that is, God with the people) represented a seismic shift. A sung, solemn high Latin Mass inspires passive contemplation of transcendent mystery; the contemporary liturgy in the vernacular invites active celebration of the Incarnation and participation in the paschal mystery. Both have their place.

When the "Word became flesh" (John 1:14), Jesus reconsecrated all that is authentically human. Instead of God's revelation coming to humans as had been done in ages past, God now communicates through a human. Our humanity, redeemed in Christ, has become the new temple through which we encounter the divine. The incarnation of Christ compels us to take our human nature seriously, because God does. We share with God a common vocation: becoming human.

The sublime echoes of Gregorian chant and Palestrina polyphony retain their pride of place in the rich treasury of Catholic sacred music. From time to time these still resound through the chapel at Maryknoll, New York. But missioners delight in gathering together people of faith around the world to worship God with their own voice and in their own tongue and using their own music. Liturgy does not just celebrate the mission of the Son of God to redeem humanity; in a real sense it continues that mission. Like a spiritual time machine joining past and future in the present moment, each Eucharist becomes an extension of the paschal mystery into this time, in this place, in this culture, and in this country.

A Kenyan girl beams with joy at her First Communion.

Drumming, dancing, singing, and women's high-pitched ululation during Mass capture the almost insuppressible joy Africans feel during Eucharist, which, without any urgency for people to get to a parking lot or to the mall or beach, may go on for several happy hours. Asians feel very much at home with silence and solemnity or more formal ritual and choral singing. The festive spirit of Latin America permeates liturgical gatherings in that part of the world, especially during fiestas for patron saints and celebrations for Holy Week.

Catholic liturgy often attracts the outsider to inquire about the goings-on. A missioner in Japan once noticed a Buddhist monk respectfully standing in the back of the church and observing Mass. When later greeted and asked if he had any questions, he simply replied he was fascinated by the priest's gestures, which he described as "holy."

Weddings and funerals offer singular opportunities for evangelization, to non-Catholics as well as to those "fallen away" or "lapsed." Many outside visitors comment on the solemnity of the Mass, and some cite this as their first step toward becoming Catholic. Liturgy can and should deepen or renew the faith of Catholics as well.

Liturgy must influence what we do outside as much as inside the church. The Washing of the Feet, for example, need not be confined to a once-a-year ritual on Holy Thursday. It is as much an attitude of life as it is a one-day ceremony. One Maryknoller had to arbitrate between arguing factions in the parish whose increasing hostilities threatened to destroy the entire community. After a day of heated discussion and prayer, the priest called the leaders of the opposing sides up to the auditorium stage and, in front of the entire congregation, asked them to take a seat and remove their shoes and socks. While a parishioner read aloud the appropriate passage from John's Gospel, to their surprise the priest began washing their feet and then invited them to wash each other's feet, in keeping with the command of the Lord (John 13:14). This dramatic act of humble service finally broke through the entrenched positions between the rival groups and reminded them that true leadership requires service to one another. This attitude should permeate every aspect of Christian life. No task is too menial when done out of love. The gospel lived thus becomes the gospel preached.

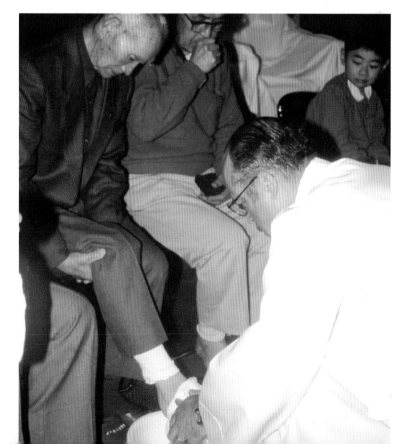

Fr. Frank Riha washes the feet of parishioners in Japan.

Fr. Ed Moffett worked on a remote island in the Yellow Sea off the east coast of Korea. One day, people came to him in desperation. A boy had fallen into a large, fifteen-foot-deep earthen pit used to collect human waste to be used as fertilizer in the rice paddies. The boy never resurfaced. Fr. Ed ran to the spot where friends saw the youngster disappear. The priest stripped down to his underwear and dove into the cesspool. He came up for air twice before locating the boy's body on the third try, to the bittersweet relief and gratitude of the parents.

The Mass, the central liturgy of the Roman Catholic Church, by nature and by definition is ordered toward mission. The word "Mass" itself comes from the final Latin phrase at the close of the liturgy, *"Ite, Missa est."* Popular interpretation renders this as "Go, the Mass is ended," but the original meaning was more dynamic: "Go, it is sent." In other words, the Word of God made flesh in Jesus and celebrated in this Eucharist is now sent out into the world through you. Catholicism's highest form of worship impels the faithful to go; indeed, it sends us out into the world, even if it's just to our own neighborhood, to spread the Good News. Instructed by the Word of God and empowered by the Body of Christ (Eucharist), the Body of Christ (people of God) lives out their baptismal vocations by becoming missioners.

Proclamation

Proclamation is at once the easiest and most difficult aspect of mission. Long gone are the days when Maryknoll seminarians and Brother candidates would go down to Times Square and literally stand on a soapbox and preach the Word of God to bemused, confused, or apathetic, if not antagonistic, passers-by. Summer street preaching in the Southern Baptist Bible Belt of Alabama prepared earlier Maryknollers for the opposition they could expect overseas. Father Price honed his preaching skills in just such a hostile anti-Catholic environment in his home state of North Carolina. Once, while Price was street preaching, a heckler shouted out at him, "What's the difference between a priest and a horse's ass?" Without missing a beat, Price responded, "Why don't you come stand next to me and we can show these good people the difference?"

As gratifying as such legends may be, it's hard to say if it resulted in anyone's conversion. Besides, that was in a very different century. Experience teaches us that one-to-one faith sharing proves more effective, albeit less personally satisfying and dramatic, than shouting the Good News above the Midtown din in competition with secular or even other religious distractions—or getting the upper hand on a Protestant heckler. That being said, in recent years one Maryknoller put the Gospel of Mark to music and, while strumming his guitar, proclaimed the Good News through song to passers-by in a plaza in Santiago, Chile, as well as in Union Square in New York City. There is nothing to prevent a modern Maryknoller from

Fr. Mike Bassano
publicly proclaims
the gospel in Chile.

proclaiming the gospel in public squares and street corners as missioners have done over many generations. Maryknoll's mantra, here as in other areas, is not either/or, but both/and.

In Kujo, Japan, a man was waiting for a trolley on a traffic island when it started to rain. He ducked into a vestibule of a Maryknoll church for shelter, and through the closed doors he overheard a homily by Fr. John J. Walsh. An American speaking in Japanese about God and Jesus dying for our sins made an impact. The man was so moved, he not only converted to Catholicism, he became a Trappist monk.

Directly announcing the reign of God and the availability of God's love, forgiveness, mercy, and salvation to all people seems easier when done through mass media. Perhaps this is because magazines, radio, TV, and videos offer a comfortable buffer from people's disapproving or hostile questions or outright opposition. Maryknoll's founders appreciated the power of the written word to disseminate Catholic truth. Walsh and Price were both publishers of Catholic papers before they joined forces to form Maryknoll. Rogers and the first Sisters not only helped bundle and mail out early issues of *The Field Afar,* Maryknoll magazine's original title, Rogers actually ghostwrote many editorials on Walsh's behalf. They realized that, unlike the spoken word, the written word takes on a life of its own, extending its power to edify and inspire long after those who wrote it are gone while finding new readers years and even decades later.

Maryknoll's publications and programs continue the Maryknoll spirit of inclusion, seeking truth no matter where it comes from and listening respectfully to opposing or dissenting points of view.

In keeping with this spirit of the founders, Maryknoll continues to proclaim the good news not only through its magazines, but also through radio (*Voices of Our World*), DVDs and videos (*The Field Afar* and *Children of the Earth* series), and Orbis Books, not to mention its websites www.maryknoll.org and www.livesofservice.org, as well as weekly email prayers, Facebook pages, and Twitter.

Witness

The expression "speaking truth to power" comes to us from the Quakers. They made headlines in the 1960s when they invoked their religious beliefs as grounds for opposing war. Their nonviolent witness conjures up the image of Christ before Pontius Pilate. Jesus, bound and bruised but unbowed, stands his ground before the Roman governor. From a purely materialistic point of view, Pilate is in power and appears to have the upper hand. The story should have ended with the execution of Jesus, but it doesn't. Twenty centuries later, the birth of the Victim divides the dates of the Roman Empire between BC and AD. Every Sunday, more than 2 billion Christians worldwide confess their faith in the true Victor, who spoke truth to power and who "suffered under Pontius Pilate."

Saints throughout the ages found strength to witness for the faith. Indeed, the word "martyr" comes from the Greek for "witness." Paradoxically, martyrs, prophets, and reformers at times received as much opposition from fellow believers and leaders of the Church as from the secular world, as predicted by Jesus: "One's enemies will be those of one's own household" (Matthew 10:36). St. Francis of Assisi was expelled from the Franciscans. St. Ignatius of Loyola saw his Jesuit order suppressed by the Church for a time. St. Joan of Arc was burned as a witch by an English ecclesial court. In a word, witnesses make waves. They rock the boat, including the bark of Peter.

Besides witnessing to the world, certain saints at times also witnessed against excesses in the Church. Many reforms within Catholicism occurred because of brave souls such as St. Teresa of Avila. For her reform efforts she faced opposition within her own Carmelite order and was even brought up on charges before the Roman Inquisition. Today we acknowledge her as a Doctor of the Church as well as one of Maryknoll's patron saints.

Throughout its one hundred years, Maryknoll has had its share of witnesses, some very public, others rather personal. In the 1980s, when drought threw East Africa into acute famine, the people looked for a scapegoat. Father Herbert Gappa rescued a woman whom they wanted to sacrifice for being a witch who caused the famine. During the Vietnam War, Maryknoll Father Vincent Capodanno, mentioned earlier, was killed while administering the last rites to a wounded soldier. Named

Servant of God by Pope Benedict, Capodanno's cause for canonization is supported by the U.S. military vicariate. On the opposite side of the political spectrum, Maryknoll Father Roy Bourgeois, a navy veteran, continues a decades-long witness against the human rights abuses perpetrated by graduates of the U.S.-funded School of the Americas (Western Hemisphere Institute for Security Cooperation) in Fort Benning, Georgia. Yet for his efforts promoting the ordination of women, Bourgeois incurred the severest form of disciplinary action in the Church: excommunication. More than sixty years ago, Father John Considine, M.M., decried the appalling lack of priests to administer the Eucharist and other sacraments to the vast ma-

Fr. Bob McCahill witnesses to the love of God for all people.

jority of Catholics in Latin America. His book, *Call for 40,000,* underscored the urgent need for priests and called upon the Vatican to ordain qualified men to the priesthood from among the many trained native married catechists. His prophetic witness has gone unheeded since the book came out in 1943. After the outbreak of World War II, when Japanese Americans were rounded up and placed in internment camps, several Maryknoll missioners stayed with them. Father Alfred Keane's testimony before Congress was instrumental in getting the U.S. government to grant priority citizenship to the thousands of "mixed blood" offspring of U.S. servicemen in Korea. When a decades-long civil war threatened the survival of many Guatemalan Indians, Brother Martin Shea witnessed to the unfailing love of God by accompanying them into exile and living with them in the refugee camps. A Maryknoller in Bangladesh, where proselytizing is against the law, nonetheless makes the gospel visible to his Muslim neighbors in need of help by treating the sick poor. Overseas, Maryknollers witness to their own faith; back home they bear witness to the faith of others.

Interreligious Dialogue

To many people, the word "missionary" still evokes images of black-robed Westerners planting crosses on pagan soil, toppling idols, and overturning an altar or two. To emphasize a new, mutually respectful way of relating to people of other faiths, Maryknoll's founders early on preferred to

be called missioners. In 1918 the morality and inner goodness of the Chinese people impressed the first Maryknollers
to China. They acknowledged that Confucians, Buddhists,
and animists have much to teach Catholics, and such beliefs
laid the groundwork for Christianity in Asia much as the Old
Testament and the Jewish faith did in the West. Such pro-
gressive thinking, decades ahead of its time, today still provokes cries of outrage from well-meaning churchgoers who
believe the Roman Catholic Church not only possesses all
truth but also has nothing to learn from other religions. They
maintain it's the sole job of a missioner to go abroad and
make people turn Catholic. As mentioned earlier, for years
Maryknoll missioners played what they called the "numbers
game," where success was measured in how many baptisms,
Communions, and marriages one performed. While de-
ceptively quantifiable, this practice ignored the focus Jesus
placed on the mustard seed, the lost sheep, the yeast, where
results are not always so readily apparent. In recent years,
with declining numbers, Maryknollers are rediscovering, albeit begrudgingly, the call to become a small yet vital part
of the reign of God.

Following the example of Jesus, who affirmed the
faith of the Syro-Phoenician woman, the Roman centurion,
and several Samaritans—all non-Jews—Maryknollers approach other religions with profound respect. Indeed, an
openness toward and intellectual curiosity about other faiths
mark the spirit of Maryknoll.

At the heart of interreligious dialogue lies the conviction that God works through all peoples of faith, who respond to God's grace in their own way. Fruitful dialogue begins when we acknowledge what we admire about another religion. The purpose of interreligious dialogue, from Maryknoll's point of view, is not to prove Catholicism right and all other religions wrong, but rather to show how each of our respective religions can help others grow closer to God and further illuminate our own revealed truths.

As the name implies, true interreligious dialogue takes place among members of different religions. Maryknollers were especially blessed during the 1970s and 1980s to have not one but two Jewish professors on the faculty of the Maryknoll School of Theology. Rabbi Asher Finkel not only taught Torah, Psalms, and Prophets, he also introduced the students and seminarians to the Passover Seder, which Jesus celebrated as his last supper. Rabbi Finkel also helped them appreciate the teachings of Rabbi Jesus of Nazareth from a Jewish point of view. Jewish theologian Mark Ellis taught peace and justice and articulated the plight of Palestinians in Israel. Professor Ralph Bultjens, a Buddhist from Sri Lanka, brought his religion's insights of detachment and mindfulness into the classroom. Such openness to welcoming as well as listening to differing points of view is another aspect that marks the Maryknoll spirit.

For Maryknollers working in Muslim countries in Egypt, Indonesia, or Bangladesh, interreligious dialogue takes the form of a "dialogue of life." Muslim neighbors and colleagues show the utmost respect for the Catholic missioner

among them as being a man of God. One Maryknoller visited a Muslim family in Egypt during the holy month of Ramadan, when Muslims fast during daylight hours. Despite their custom of not eating, they nonetheless happily prepared a full meal for their guest and watched as he almost apologetically partook both of their food and their hospitality.

Fr. Bill McCarthy shares insights with Buddhists.

Interreligious dialogue can have its downside, if not its limits. While what unites us is important, our differences are crucial. In Bangladesh a missioner, the only Christian for hundreds of miles, was well liked and respected among his Muslim neighbors. He said his prayers and Masses privately in his small hut and helped people attend to the poor who needed medical attention. If anyone asked why he was there, he did not hesitate to say his love for Jesus compelled him. Muslims respect Jesus as a great prophet and so accepted his answer. Over the years he cultivated many close friendships. One in particular was with a Muslim professor, who came over regularly for afternoon tea and theological discussions. One day the professor asked point-blank, "Who is Jesus for you?" In an instant, the mission context changed from interreligious dialogue to one of witness and proclamation. He replied, "Jesus is the Son of God." The missioner recounts with some sadness how his friend's face suddenly lost all color. He stood up, leaving his tea untouched, and walked away never to return. Such encounters with other religions help Maryknollers think about their own religious convictions.

After a grueling day at his work in Tanzania one Christmas, Br. Kevin Dargan looked forward to a quiet supper of canned sardines, smoked oysters, and Spam from the States. A knock at the door interrupted his solitary meal. A Muslim neighbor had noticed his situation, told his wife, and she sent over a home-cooked meal, saying, "Nobody should celebrate Christmas eating out of tin cans."

Unlike interreligious dialogue, ecumenism seeks to find common ground among Christian denominations, our proverbial "separated brethren." The yearly "Octave for Christian Unity" comes to the Universal Church from the Franciscan Society of the Atonement, just a few miles north of Maryknoll, New York, but the closeness between the two Societies is more than geographical. Their founder, Father Paul Wattson, a close friend of Maryknoll cofounder Father James A. Walsh, met frequently with him to discuss the fledgling mission Society. Wattson and his group had converted from Anglicanism a few years before and no doubt imbued Maryknoll from the beginning with a deep respect for other Christian denominations.

With ecumenism, each Christian group in its own way and life emphasizes different aspects of what it means to be followers of Christ. Eastern Orthodox liturgies celebrate the transcendent wisdom and glory of God with mystical solemnity; Quakers promote pacifism and nonviolence as mentioned earlier; Mennonites and Amish are known for simplicity of lifestyle. There is also the great emphasis Protestant denominations in general place on the Bible and preaching, the centrality of strong family ties by the Mormons, the missionary zeal of the Evangelicals to spread the faith, as well as the Pentecostals to manifest the gifts of the Holy Spirit.

The Maryknoll spirit compels its members to approach Christians and followers of other faiths not so much as rivals or adversaries but as co-seekers of the Truth. What makes one's religion "true" is proven more by life and witness than by academic debate.

Human Development

Maryknoll cofounder Bishop James A. Walsh summed up the Maryknoll spirit in one word: charity. "If there is any other spirit," he wrote in the Maryknoll Spiritual Directory, "we don't want it." Charity holds pride of place among the so-called evangelical counsels, along with chastity and obedience, as the mark of a disciple of Christ. St. Paul ranks it ahead of faith and hope (1 Corinthians 13:13). Some religious circles interpret this as "poverty" in the sense of total giving of oneself and one's resources for the community and, by extension, for others. The word "charity" hardly captures the dynamic, self-sacrificing meaning of the Greek word for love: agape. Christian charity does not so much call for largesse in doing things to or for the poor out of one's abundance, but rather for a radical, simplified lifestyle in order to share with others the essentials of life.

A twelve-year old boy in Mindanao, Philippines, who'd lost his father years earlier, now found himself an orphan when his mother died in a motorcycle accident. His aunt took him in, but they received no compensation from the driver of the motorcycle. Fr. Bob Depinet began to support the struggling family to see them through the hard times. The boy couldn't understand the priest's charity and asked his aunt, "Why is Father Bob helping us? He wasn't the one responsible."

When people think of Maryknoll they first think of mission, followed by peace and justice. Throughout its existence, Maryknoll has confronted issues such as war, the environment, and equal rights impelled by the love of Christ. In recent decades, some people have criticized Maryknoll for being what they perceive as too political. By this, they mean missioners should stick to making converts and saving souls. Ironically, these same people do not hesitate to encourage clergy to get involved politically and pressure Congress when they agree with the issue at hand.

By and large, Maryknoll missioners reject a dualistic view of the world that separates human activity into religious and secular. Jesus, after all, both truly human and truly divine, lived in the world. He was born in a stable, not in the temple. He used everyday human activities as parables for the reign of God. Ultimately, he was executed by the Romans as a political threat to the political, economic, and militaristic Roman Empire. The sign above his cross read *"Iesus Nazarenus Rex Iudeorum"*— Jesus of Nazareth, king of the Jews, a political charge of treason.

  MIRRORS OF GRACE

In recent decades Maryknoll strongly opposed NAFTA (the North American Free Trade Agreement) on the grounds it would have an adverse effect on the economy and workers of Mexico, as well as result in lost jobs in the United States. Maryknoll supports the U.S. bishops' call for just treatment of undocumented aliens in the United States and for comprehensive immigration reform. Maryknoll continues to advocate for equitable treatment for Palestinians, the signing of the Kyoto Protocol on global warming and the environment, not to mention expressing opposition to the wars in Iraq and Afghanistan, costing so much in money and human lives and suffering.

In many circles these positions are highly controversial. Never mind that Pope John Paul II called the Iraq war a "defeat for humanity" and Pope Benedict denounced the policy of "preemptive war"; some Catholics criticized Maryknoll as political, if not treasonous, because missioners dared publicly question and challenge the policies of our government. For Maryknollers, the call to live and proclaim the gospel and to seek change that benefits the poor does not alter with the party in power.

Christianity cares for the body as well as the soul. Catholicism, in particular, has always emphasized the need to make faith visible through concrete acts of charity (James 1:17). Charity can take many forms, from individual generosity to more ambitious and far-reaching relief or development programs. Such concern for the physical as well as the spiritual well-being of people flows naturally from the belief in the Incarnation.

Jesus did not save only our souls, he sanctified the entire human person. Missioners recognize that every aspect of human life—social, economic, psychological, intellectual, political, as well as spiritual—must be transformed and perfected by the gospel. True God, Jesus was totally human like us in all things but sin. The more we eradicate sin from our lives, the more like Jesus we become. The more like Jesus people become, the more they reflect God. Here is the motivation for mission.

Because Maryknollers take the Incarnation seriously, much conflict and controversy arise. Few Catholics would deny the Church's right to take a very public and vocal stand opposing abortion, even though this has very obvious political consequences. The Church denounces any form of so-called progress predicated on the need to destroy the most vulnerable among us, in this case, the unborn child. Motivated by the gospel, many Christians take actions that invariably and inevitably have political implications. But these are not limited to protesting abortions. A Maryknoller's pro-life stance also includes what happens to people after they are born. This is the so-called seamless garment approach to life first articulated by the late Cardinal Joseph Bernardin of Chicago. It states that all human life deserves respect and protection, from natural conception to natural death and all phases in between. Conversely, the gospel demands we strongly oppose anything that dehumanizes people, from addictions to unsafe working conditions, to unjust wages, to human trafficking.

Few would deny that the political spheres of human interaction are sorely in need of repentance and conversion. But that is not Maryknoll's primary purpose. Concern for authentic human development goes way beyond this limited

scope. Active interest in the physical, economic, and emotional health of people as an integral part of their spiritual salvation inspires missioners to become involved in all sorts of
human development projects. The bricks-and-mortar side of
mission is obvious, with many buildings around the world still
bearing Maryknoll's name even though missioners no longer
work there, such as the Maryknoll Hospital in Busan, Korea,
or the many Maryknoll schools in Hawaii. Indeed, one of the
objectives marking the Maryknoll spirit in regard to building
projects has been to make it financially self-sustaining and
to turn it over to local administration—be it a parish, school,
hospital, or clinic—as soon as feasible.

*Fr. Richard Albertine
holds an outdoor
meeting in Namibia.*

So closely has mission been identified with charity in
the past that a backlash of sorts arose against creating so-called
rice Christians, especially, as the name suggests, in Asia.
Following the devastation of world and regional wars and
revolutions, well-meaning Christian missionaries poured into
refugee areas with relief goods. To be sure, many people expressed their gratitude by joining the Church. Some remained,

yet many others fell away once supplies ran out, the need passed, or a better source of support surfaced. Interestingly enough, when Jesus says to "make friends for yourself with unrighteous mammon" (Luke 16:9), he did not suggest giving away money and material goods as a way to win converts, but rather, "when they [resources] fail they [friends] may receive you into an everlasting home." True Christian charity benefits both giver and receiver.

Given a chance, Tanzanians will flourish.

Other aspects of human development are far less tangible but no less important. Literacy programs, community workshops, and leadership seminars all play an integral part in evangelizing the human person and the society in which

he or she lives, thus fulfilling the words of St. Irenaeus: "The glory of God is the human being totally alive." Yet here, too, misunderstanding and opposition arise. One Maryknoller was expelled from Honduras in the 1980s. His crime? Teaching workers about their country's own constitution and labor laws.

In recent decades more and more Maryknollers have become involved in various movements to protect the environment. Sustainable development in poorer countries, a more equitable sharing of the Earth's resources, moving away from dependence on fossil fuels, and global warming are not distractions from Maryknoll's primary purpose of mission. Maryknoll sees these as an extension and, indeed, a fulfillment of Christ's mandate to preach the Good News to all creation (Mark 16:15).

An amateur birder, Fr. George Cotter installed a birdbath behind his house in Debre Zeit, Ethiopia. He enjoyed watching the various species of birds in the area. One day, he and a visitor sat on the porch wondering about an unusual chirping they heard. They concluded it must be a rarely seen woodpecker found only in that part of the world. After the visitor left, Fr. George went inside and discovered the source of the chirping: his computer was signaling that the battery was low.

God became human on this Earth. Jesus walked on the ground, breathed the air, drank the water. Every cell of his body was taken from our Earth. This compels Maryknollers—indeed all Christians—to be as respectful of the Earth as we are of the bread and wine that become the Body and Blood of Christ.

"And they devoted themselves to the apostles' teaching and the fellowship, to the breaking of bread and the prayers."
—Acts 2:42

"And let us consider how to stir up one another to love and good works, not neglecting to meet together, as is the habit with some, but encouraging one another."
—Hebrews 10:24

Chapter Four

Catholic Foreign Mission SOCIETY of America

B eing a Society of Apostolic Life means Maryknoll focuses its attention, energy, and resources on its main charism: overseas mission. For Maryknollers, mission takes precedence over community life and even prayer. In the Church, Maryknoll priests are neither "fish nor fowl." That is, Maryknoll is not a religious Order like the Franciscans, Benedictines, Augustinians, or Dominicans who follow an established Rule and live in community; neither is it strictly speaking secular. Canonically, Maryknoll Fathers are diocesan priests, and the Brothers are celibate laymen who have come together for one specific purpose: overseas mission. They may be assigned anywhere in the world where their service or presence is needed, including the United States, but their purpose is to promote mission.

Prior to ordination, deacons take a vow of celibacy, but unlike men in religious Orders, Maryknollers do not take solemn vows of poverty, chastity, and obedience. Rather, seminarians or Brother candidates in formation take a series of annual, temporary oaths and then a permanent oath to "the work of the missions . . . and to uphold the Constitutions of the Society and to obey [their] legitimate superiors." At Maryknoll, New York, a custom has arisen where, at the funeral of a missioner, his permanent oath is read publicly one last time as a meditation following Communion while the congregation sings, "Jesus, remember me, when you come into your kingdom." This final tribute attests to the Maryknoller's having faithfully fulfilled his oath to dedicate his "whole life to the work of the missions."

Unintentional Community

Community and communal living have never been Maryknoll's strong suit. On the contrary, the myth of the "rugged individual" has long inspired (some would say plagued) missioners for much of Maryknoll's existence. One admirer half-jokingly suggested that John Wayne be numbered among Maryknoll's patron saints. Indeed, a Japanese friend of one missioner described Maryknollers as a "pack of lone wolves." A Maryknoll Sister who worked for decades with the Fathers on the missions called them "popes unto themselves." In the past, rarely did more than two Mary-

knollers live and work together in mission, and if they did, the pastor or "local superior" called the shots. More often than not, a Maryknoller was alone on his mission, save for perhaps a hundred thousand local people. The morale of a missioner sometimes seems in inverse proportion to his proximity to other Maryknollers. The farther they lived from one another, the happier they were.

Fr. Ken Sleymann teaches medical ethics in Japan.

None other than Bishop James E. Walsh, prior to his twenty-year sentence to house arrest and solitary confinement in China, in his Description of a Missioner, commented how a missioner's worst enemy was usually "the Maryknoller sitting across from him at the breakfast table." Other bromides abound. "The only thing worse than being alone on the missions is living with another Maryknoller." "Wherever two or more Maryknollers are gathered together, they are talking about the fourth." To be fair, such attitudes characterize older members more than younger ones. Maryknoll Brothers, in fact, have always placed a higher priority on community and hospitality than do the Fathers, desiring, as far as possible, to be assigned to a mission with another Brother. Paradoxically, when meetings or assemblies call Maryknollers together from fields afar, the men seem genuinely happy to see each other and enjoy one another's company.

Words such as "team," "consensus," and worst of all, "sharing" gained currency in recent years and only then with suspicion on the part of some missioners. Men who entered since the 1960s felt more at home in community and actively sought it out, especially overseas, either with fellow Maryknollers or with other foreign missioners or local priests, religious, or laypeople. These "younger" members, however, remain outnumbered by the vast majority of Maryknollers for whom the image of the "wounded hero" remains an inspiration.

Shrinking numbers and advancing age, however, have foisted on retired and semiretired missioners a communal lifestyle for which most are ill-prepared, untrained, and unwilling participants. The Maryknoll Fathers and Brothers headquarters in Ossining, New York, is arguably the largest concentration of priests and Brothers living under one roof in the world. With close to one hundred residents, life in this involuntary community challenges members more than any hardship encountered overseas, emotionally if not physically. Men who spent their lives alone in foreign mission have a very difficult time adjusting to doing nothing together at home. They feel their very identities and ideas of self-worth are undermined. The challenge is to do for one another what they did for others: share the good news of Jesus Christ. This puts to the ultimate test Maryknoll's guiding principle to be "temporary, mobile, and flexible." One retired Maryknoller observed that at his advanced age, the only thing temporary, mobile, and flexible about him is his theology.

Humor

When Maryknollers do get together, whether young or old, at home or abroad, you can count on spirited conversation on any range of topics, quick repartee, and plenty of jokes. A Tanzanian commented on how he could always tell when he was approaching a Maryknoll compound in Africa by the joyous laughter that rang out. Mother Mary Joseph included "the saving grace of a sense of humor" in her description of a Maryknoll Sister, but this surely applies to all Maryknollers as well.

Mistakes in foreign language pronunciation have kept Maryknollers humble and peoples overseas amused nigh these many years: the missioner to Korea who mispronounced "Immaculate Conception" as the feast of "Mary without a girdle"; the priest in Brazil who learned to his chagrin only after Mass ended that he did not say he had enjoyed a delicious regional dish but rather that he had devoured a pregnant woman; the Maryknoller in Tanzania who fell off his motorcycle—twice—on his way to a chapel for Mass and tried to explain in Kiswahili to the parishioners he was limping because he "fell" from his bike. He couldn't understand their laughter and total lack of sympathy until he realized he'd told them he was limping because he had "hatched an egg." Of course, the funniest or most embarrassing things that have happened to Maryknollers over the years cannot usually be shared in polite company. But for a delightful evening, ask a Maryknoller to share from his collection of unusual anecdotes.

After eight years of teaching English in China, Fr. Tom Wilcox made an attempt to write the two Chinese characters for "beautiful" and "country," which together mean "America" in Mandarin. He showed his work to a student who remarked, "That's the way I did it in nursery school."

Two things Maryknollers have learned from experience over the years: the physical and emotional strains of mission life, the isolation, the disappointments, the frustrations, the setbacks, and even at times the failures—not to mention the extreme situations of violence, war, disease, and poverty—require both a steady prayer life and a keen sense of humor. Without these a missioner is not going to survive, much less maintain his sanity.

The Body Politic

Maryknollers are by no means monolithic when it comes to politics. The Society's overall liberal (some might say radical) reputation aside, Maryknollers espouse widely divergent political views, although, truth be told, a member with deep-seated conservative proclivities may feel outnumbered or besieged much of the time. Yet Maryknollers strive to be as respectful and accepting of differing opinions among their fellow missioners as they are of other people's ideas. This only adds to the possibility of lively discussions, if not the rare shouting match, between more passionate partisans on controversial topics, not unlike what may occur at any family reunion. On the other hand, there is an unwritten practice that when a member lands in hot water overseas and gets himself expelled by the foreign authorities for pushing the political envelope too far, Maryknollers close ranks in solidarity, offering moral support for the man if not for his actions or positions.

Father Joe La Mar represents the Maryknoll Fathers and Brothers as an entity joining forces with many other like-minded religious groups to form the Interfaith Committee for Corporate Social Responsibility. They lobby—or sue—businesses to obey international laws promoting human rights, fair labor practices, and environmental issues. By voting their combined shares at shareholders' meetings or by taking companies to court, this group has successfully forced Pepsi and Texaco out of Myanmar (Burma) after the military overthrew the democratically elected president; they pressured Unocal

Fr. Ben Zweber gives the Body of Christ to Koreans.

Oil Company to include human rights considerations in dealing with foreign countries; and they got Freeport McMoRan to reverse life-threatening pollution practices in their gold, silver, and copper mines in Indonesia. In all things, the governing principle is to put human beings first and to evaluate all programs and policies on what effect they have on the lives of ordinary people, especially the poor. For Maryknoll, the bottom line is people over profits.

Despite their individual differences, Society members beautifully express loyalty and support for one another in the long-standing tradition of making every effort to attend the funeral of a parent or close relative of a fellow Maryknoller. Besides the consolation and spiritual comfort afforded the family by seeing many concelebrants around the altar or missioners in the pews, more than one observer has commented on how inspiring it sounded, hearing strong male voices belting out Catholic hymns. Singing is not uncommon at Maryknoll gatherings. Not that they come close to being professionals, Maryknollers gamely belt out tunes and supply improvised harmonies, with volume and spirit if not always accuracy.

While their oath binds them to one another as a Society, smaller voluntary groupings based on interests or mission areas flourish within Maryknoll. Pastoral Theological Reflection (PTR)—when men get together on a regular basis overseas to pray, read Scripture, and share experiences—has continued back at the Center as well. Other support or interest groups form or disband as need rises or falls.

The three times Maryknollers can always be counted on to gather on a regular basis in any appreciable numbers are for Mass, meals, and meetings. Televised sporting events may also give missioners an excuse to congregate who would not normally socialize together—whether for World Cup, World Series, or Wonderful World of Sumo Wrestling—since underneath it all, Maryknollers are American males.

The dining room at the Center offers a beautiful symbol of the Maryknoll spirit in miniature. The many round tables provide an expression of Maryknoll's inclusive and egalitarian nature. With five chairs for each round table, the men occasionally squeeze in a sixth or even seventh place at the table, so all might have a place. Lacking a head of the table, everyone is equal. It would not be uncommon to find a visitor seated with assorted Maryknollers, a seminarian and perhaps even a bishop, most if not all in civilian clothes. Whoever happens to get up for dessert or coffee may clear away the dirty dishes, much to the surprise—if not embarrassment, but, one hopes, edification—of the guest. Thus, a bishop may be as likely as a seminarian to take away the plates, glasses, and silverware. Such quiet and unassuming service highlights an integral part of the Maryknoll spirit. While mindful and respectful of rank, few Maryknollers pull it.

It is not uncommon for the U.S. Embassy to invite all the expats in the country to come to the embassy compound for a cookout on the Fourth of July. One ambassador in Latin America said he could always distinguish two groups from among

the hundreds of guests: Peace Corps volunteers and Mary-
knollers. Peace Corps volunteers, he observed, were the ones
clustered around the Swedish meatballs; Maryknollers were
the ones always talking with the staff.

As mentioned earlier, absent a religious habit or mandatory Mass and prayer times, Maryknoll's individual lifestyles
are as varied as its members. Some are very faithful to praying the Divine Office (breviary) daily, alone if necessary but
with others when possible. Some men may not have picked
up their breviaries since seminary days. While many make
an effort to attend the daily community liturgy, a few men
may gather for Mass at a different time in one of several small
chapels around the Center. An older priest might even elect
to say daily Mass by himself at one of the few remaining side
altars in the crypt, not quite convinced or comfortable with
this newfangled concept of concelebration.

Because they do not take a vow of poverty, Maryknollers may own personal property, inherited or earned.
Some men have their own cars and bank accounts. A communal TV room provides an opportunity to gather for entertain-
ment, but the man who gets there first commands use of the
all-important remote control. This might explain why there
are so many personal TVs in private rooms. For the Society
as a whole, a "spirit of poverty" has ebbed and flowed over
the course of decades, with "stewardship" of resources acting
as the overarching, moderating factor. Simplicity of lifestyle
still seems ingrained in most missioners, who may suffer

Nepali villagers greet Fr. Joe Thaler with flowers and "Namaste!" ("I salute the devine in you.")

in silence at what they perceive as extravagant expenses or waste by the Society or by fellow members. Of course, being Maryknollers, such silence seldom lasts.

So strong and deeply ingrained is the Maryknoll spirit that it may remain long after a man has left the Society. It keeps members interested in the lives of those men who have left, whether to marry or to incardinate (join a diocese) or enter another religious community. Maryknoll hosts an annual gathering of "formers" and their wives or partners, where friendships renew or continue. A quarterly publication called *Interchange* keeps former members up to date on news from the "Knoll" as well as with the lives of individuals who have left. The "Chi Ro" fund is maintained by former members to help one another adjust to life outside of Maryknoll. It is not unusual for former members who have become financially successful to join the ranks of Maryknoll's generous benefactors. Of course, depending a great deal on the circumstances surrounding their leaving Maryknoll, some former members simply "fall off the radar screen" and are not seen nor heard from again. They cut off all ties with the Society and make no attempt to communicate their whereabouts or well-being, but this is always at their initiative.

Hospitality

Nothing reflects the Maryknoll spirit better than hospitality, in its various forms. In the *Maryknoll Spiritual Directory*, Bishop James E. Walsh placed hospitality even above private prayer. He reasoned that a missioner does not go overseas to pray his Office or the rosary. Rather, a Maryknoller goes abroad specifically to engage in person-to-person conversations about matters of faith. Walsh thus reminds missioners that nothing is more important than the unexpected guest. Walsh admonishes Maryknollers even to interrupt their prayer and attend to the unannounced visitor who, unbeknownst, fulfills the very reason the missioner is overseas.

Perhaps because they know what it feels like to be strangers in a strange land and be welcomed into an unfamiliar house, Maryknollers go out of their way to help visitors

The Asmat man of Irian Jaya, Indonesia, paints Fr. Vince Cole with tribal colors.

feel at home. Having so many members who have lived in so many different lands, a guest visiting Maryknoll headquarters from abroad may very likely be greeted in his or her native tongue. Indeed, precisely because missioners are focused outward, the very presence of guests and visitors seems to rekindle Maryknollers' enthusiasm and spirit.

A Brazilian priest joined Fr. Dennis Moorman and other Maryknollers for lunch and mentioned it was not unusual for the people to invite priests over for a home-cooked meal. However, one time when he was visiting a family close to suppertime, he could smell the delicious aromas wafting from the kitchen and so asked one of the children, "What time do you eat supper?" In stark honesty the youngster replied, "Mom says we're going to eat just as soon as you leave."

"For our citizenship is in heaven, from which we also
eagerly wait for a Savior, the Lord Jesus Christ."
—Philippians 3:20

"For here we have no lasting city,
but we seek the city which is to come."
—Hebrews 13:14

Chapter Five

Catholic Foreign Mission Society of AMERICA

E ver since the Emperor Constantine legalized Christianity
in AD 313, and the Emperor
Theodosius made it the official religion of the Roman and
Byzantine Empire in 325, mission activity went hand-in-glove
with imperial conquest and expansion. Colonial powers
encouraged and exploited the missionary zeal of religious
Orders to go to the ends of the earth. With the discovery of the
new world by Christian Europe in 1492, the Church enjoyed a
dramatic upsurge in evangelization efforts. Missionaries
sought new souls to save, even as European monarchs envi-
sioned new lands and peoples to conquer and exploit. Neither
Church nor State doubted or questioned the superiority of Western civilization or the premise that such colonial expansion was

anything less than the will of God. The one notable exception was Father Bartolomé de las Casas, a Dominican missionary to Mexico and Peru who published a book boldly documenting and deploring the enslavement of Africans and mistreatment of Indians by Spanish colonists in the Americas—at a time when European churchmen debated whether or not Indians and black people had souls. Only recently has the work and witness of de las Casas been recognized by the Church enough to advance his cause for sainthood.

The fledgling Maryknoll Society caught the first wave of U.S. emergence on the world stage as a superpower. With atheistic communism overtaking Russia in 1917 and Nazism infecting Germany and threatening world peace in the 1930s, the United States assumed the role of defender of democracy and freedom for the world. Maryknoll was ready to assist that effort in whatever way it could. It is no coincidence that the greatest upswing in vocations to Maryknoll occurred in the years immediately following the United States leading the Allies to victory in the Second World War in 1945. Until as late as 1970, it was not uncommon to have ordination classes of upward of forty priests every year. Everything pointed to continued growth for the country and Maryknoll.

Occurring simultaneously in the 1960s, Vatican II and the Vietnam War delivered a double body blow to Catholics in the United States. What the former did to challenge the notion that the Roman Catholic Church never changed, the latter did to undermine confidence in the superiority—if not absolute righteousness—of U.S. foreign policy. In those

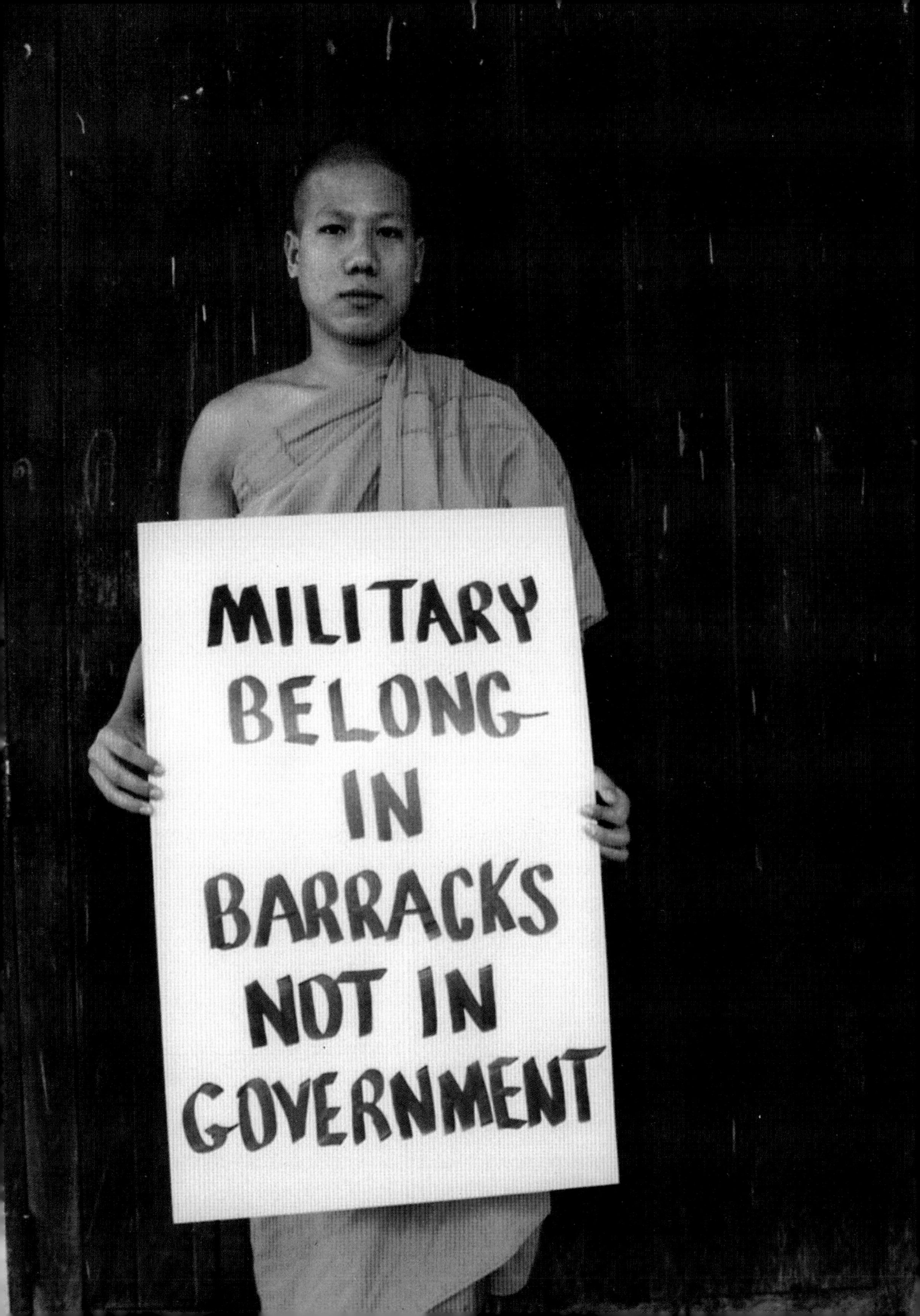
MILITARY
BELONG
IN
BARRACKS
NOT IN
GOVERNMENT

turbulent years, a disconnect began between Maryknollers and the country from whose church they had come. For every military chaplain Maryknoll supplied, there was an equal if not greater number of war protesters among its ranks.

More and more individual Maryknollers and the Society as a whole began to question publicly the wisdom and morality, let alone legality, of many U.S. actions overseas from Central and South America, to South Korea, to the Philippines. Dictators, set up and defended by the United States, began to consider missioners' work among poor people as subversive. For the first time since the Emperor Constantine, the superpower could no longer depend on missionaries to automatically bless and support its policies abroad. The unholy alliance between religious missioners and secular empire that had survived and flourished for more than eighteen hundred years had come to an end.

A Maryknoll employee approached Fr. Leo Shea and asked if he had attended the annual march in November to close the School of the Americas in Fort Benning, Georgia, where some of Latin America's worst dictators and military officers had been trained. When he learned the priest had protested the SOA, the man said, "Padre, I am from Uruguay, and I lived under military dictatorship. I know what it was like. Thank you for going."

Maryknollers remain nonetheless very much of America. They cherish American values of individual liberty; justice; freedoms of speech, religion, and conscience; egalitarianism; and a pioneering, "can-do" spirit. Indeed it may even be argued that their very vocal opposition to certain government policies stems from the all-American abhorrence to tyranny. For many Maryknollers and other Americans, protest remains the highest form of patriotism. While they express skepticism and criticism of U.S. policies detrimental to the lives of the people they serve, Maryknollers embody the best of what it means to be truly American.

Internationalization?

A recurring debate among Maryknollers is whether or not to "go international" in accepting vocations to the missionary priesthood and brotherhood. One side argues the very identity of the Catholic Foreign Mission Society of America requires its members to come from the Catholic Church in the United States. The other side counters that throughout its history, Maryknoll has admitted men from overseas, many of whom never became U.S. citizens.

The Maryknoll Sisters have been international from the beginning, so for them the question is moot. The Maryknoll Fathers and Brothers, on the other hand, were expressly created by the bishops of the United States to be a mission outreach of the Catholic Church in this country. Indeed, for years the Maryknoll Society took pride in explicitly *not* taking priest or Brother candidates from the fledgling churches it helped set up, the better to cultivate native vocations. Nowadays, of course, most of those churches are fully developed.

Maryknoll requires single, Catholic men between, the ages of twenty-one and forty to have at least two years experience as an active congregant in the United States before applying to Maryknoll. Yet someone coming from an old Italian church in upstate New York or a young Korean parish in Brooklyn will have a decidedly different experience of Catholicism than, let's say, a Catholic from a country church in Indiana, or an inner-city parish in Los Angeles. America and the Church here present a mosaic of ethnicities and cultures, so just which Church in the United States does the man represent? Ironically, U.S. bishops themselves now actively recruit overseas for candidates for the priesthood in their dioceses. To what degree does Maryknoll reflect the current reality of the Church in the United States? For Maryknoll, the debate continues.

All Americans, including Native peoples, are either immigrants or descendants of immigrants. The first people to migrate to America from Asia were the ancestors of the so-called American Indians who crossed over the now-submerged land bridge from Siberia some ten thousand years ago to find and inhabit an unpopulated hemisphere, rich in natural resources and wildlife. Long before the British set foot on American soil, experiments in democracy were already taking root among Native populations, notably the six tribes of the Iroquois League. Throughout the Colonial period and up to the present time, wave after wave of immigrants came seeking

religious, political, or economic freedoms, even at the cost of depriving these same freedoms to others. It became an unfortunate pattern that the newest arrivals to American shores suffered discrimination at the hands of the very ones who themselves suffered discrimination years, if not decades, before. American history became a checkered tapestry of struggles for survival and freedom against a backdrop of oppression, ethnic tensions, and racial strife.

Fr. Brian Barrons has a communications ministry in China.

Maryknoll's ethnic roots are decidedly Irish. Its first seven superior generals were of Irish descent. Yet even from the days of the founders, Maryknoll reached out and accepted men from other ethnicities and races. When segregation was still the law of the land in the United States, Maryknoll integrated its membership with African Americans, but not without tension. To be sure, individual behavior did not always keep up with official policy. Men of Italian, Polish, German, and in recent years Hispanic, Vietnamese, Korean, and Haitian descent occasionally experienced insensitive comments from fellow Maryknollers of other races or backgrounds. Maryknoll struggles with the concept of racial and ethnic equality, along with the rest of the country, yet solidarity with oppressed people forms the very heart of the Maryknoll spirit. So, for example, when the United States rounded up Japanese Americans into detention camps following the attack on Pearl Harbor, Maryknoll missioners received permission to accompany the people into the camps and to live there and minister to them for the duration of the war.

As the genealogies of Jesus as recorded by Matthew and Luke show, our Savior descended from a long line of sinners no less than saints, of scoundrels no less than statesmen. In similar fashion the noble American myth gradually emerged from a less than pure bloodline, tainted by injustices and inequality. In all this, Maryknoll reflects America. We are the product of our past, but we needn't let this imprison the future. By acknowledging faults and facing fears, we can liberate ourselves and our world from the vicious cycle of repeated mistakes and unconfessed failures. As American Catholics, Maryknollers strive to remove the log from the eyes of both our Church and our country, the better to see and help others remove the speck from their eyes (Matthew 7:4–5).

Pioneering Spirit

Long before *Star Trek* and Trekkies, Maryknollers prided themselves in "going where no man has gone before." Time was when Maryknoll willingly accepted mission regions precisely because no other mission society wanted to go there. Thus, Maryknollers gamely forged into the cold, barren wasteland known as the *altiplano* (high plain) of Bolivia and Peru, as well as the sweltering jungle region of the Beni, not only because they were the most harsh but because that's where people most needed ministry. What group other than Maryknoll would officially end its decades-long commitment in Hawaii the same year it opened a new mission in Siberia?

On his first trip out to his new mission out in the Chilean countryside, Fr. Ernie Lukaschek, absent a tent, found it safer to sleep in his truck. The next morning he asked a passing campesino farmer where he might find a toilet. Gesturing to the surrounding trees, the farmer said, "Take your pick."

Even as its numbers shrank, Maryknoll continued to look for new, creative ways to do ministry, seeking to become a "small but vital" mission society at service to the Universal Church. Rather than take on whole mission regions as they did in the past, Maryknollers now usually partner with other groups, nongovernmental organizations (NGOs), or the local church to take on specific works for limited time periods.

Fr. Alfonso Kim practices Zen meditation.

Ingenuity

The quintessential American trait of ingenuity served Mary-knollers well over the years. When water from the tap proved unreliable or nonexistent, missioners dug wells or spread plastic sheets over slanting roofs to catch rainwater, often warmed by solar heat and stored inside collecting barrels. They gathered the stubs of candles and, when they had enough, melted them down to make new ones. An improvised solar oven slow-roasted supper to perfection while the men were out visiting rural areas "in the bush." After mission supplies arrived in Africa from the States in huge cargo con-

tainers, the empty bins themselves served as storage space or
even a makeshift office or house. Living inside the box, Maryknollers were thinking outside the box, long before the phrase
was coined.

Individualism

What can be expected from people who use a language
that capitalizes the first-person-singular pronoun "I"?
Both the boon and bane of American society, individualism
in Maryknoll provides both blessing and curse. As mentioned in the opening chapter, in their thinking, spiritualities,
and lifestyles, Maryknollers fall somewhere in between the
no-nonsense Walsh, the eccentric Price, and the pragmatic
Rogers. So, too, depending on how much influence their
ethnic background exerts, missioners can be very group-
oriented or fiercely individualistic. Often they are a complex
combination of both. This can hinder missioners' interaction
in the Orient, where group harmony reigns supreme. Conversely, it can help missioners bring dignity to people in Asia,
Africa, and Latin America who have, by U.S. standards, little
sense of self-worth.

Being self-sufficient and a self-starter certainly has
its place on the missions. American men seem task-orient-
ed and must relearn and retune their skills and instincts
overseas where people may put a greater emphasis on the
process rather than on results. The key seems to lie in an

awareness of the thoughts and feelings of others and knowing when to submit to the often less enlightened collective will of the group.

Being by necessity and temperament so independent makes governing Maryknollers akin to herding cats. On a boat cruise up the Hudson River not far from Maryknoll headquarters, a former superior general marveled as he looked out upon the gathering of some forty-odd missioners and observed, "This is the first time I've seen so many Maryknollers going in the same direction."

Imagination

Seeing things that never were and asking "Why not?" can be a source of inspiration as well as frustration. Many Maryknollers react instinctively to situations of perceived injustice or to those that require simple common sense. When a series of droughts plagued East Africa in the 1980s causing widespread famine, vegetables in a lush Maryknoll community garden flourished, in contrast to the neighboring plots of withered crops. No mystery. The garden abutted Lake Victoria, the largest freshwater body in Africa. Yet it hadn't occurred to the people to rely on any source of water other than rain.

A Maryknoller mountain climbing with young parishioners in Korea considered the path chosen by the group leader to be unnecessarily meandering. On the descent, he followed his own observations and instincts and took a different, more direct path, arriving below long before the others. Far from receiving accolades, he was met with annoyed stares for needlessly breaking ranks with the group and causing the leader to lose face.

Still it remains the hallmark of the Maryknoll spirit not only to imagine a better world and ask "Why not?" but also to see people suffering anywhere in the world and ask "Why?"

Counterintuitive Pragmatism

As mentioned earlier, making do in a moment of need and thinking outside the box have long been American traits. This may or may not be an advantage overseas where simply getting a job done may be valued less than respecting the opinions and feelings of all those involved. In this, many a Maryknoller felt frustration overseas when the obvious took second place to the customary.

A missioner to Bolivia tried to introduce a larger, more nutritious potato to campesinos whose diets revolve around that tuber. He sought to teach by example, so he planted his garden next to theirs. At harvest he proudly displayed his larger spuds but received only sympathy from the farmers because in their minds he had failed. After all, they had produced many tiny potatoes instead of his large one.

A young man limped into the house of Fr. Gorden Fritz at the Maryknoll Indian mission in the jungles of northern Bolivia. The missioner cleaned the man's foot wound, put on ointment and a clean bandage, and told him he'd visit the next day, saying, "I don't want you walking on that foot. I expect to see the bandage as clean as it is now." The next day the missioner went to the man's dirt-floor, thatched-roof house and was shocked to see the man's foot as dirty as ever. But there, hanging on the wall, was the bandage where it could be kept clean, just as the priest had requested.

A Maryknoller took great pride in getting a well dug for villagers in Tanzania, complete with a windmill to pump water, so the women wouldn't have to spend hours walking back and forth every day to a distant pool. Grateful? Everyone hated it. The men complained the women now had too much time on their hands to get into mischief; the women complained they missed walking for water with their friends, during which they chatted and socialized.

While pragmatism is decidedly an American characteristic, there is something totally impractical about becoming a missioner overseas. For an American to become a foreign missioner is, at least in the opinion of many, counterintuitive as well as countercultural. For the most part, Maryknollers come from a country and lifestyle still the envy of many of the world's people. Missioners give up comfortable houses to live in huts; they say good-bye to their cars to ride public transportation overseas in overcrowded buses on dangerous roads;

equipped with a graduate degree, they must become like children again and learn a new language. They get exposed to exotic diseases not seen in the United States. None of this makes sense without the gospel. Paradoxically, an American giving up the good life in the States to live with, among, and like people overseas provides the most effective, and therefore practical, witness a Maryknoller can offer.

Hearing loud shouting from villagers on opposite banks of a river in Irian Jaya, Indonesia, Fr. Vince Cole thought warfare had erupted over sabotaged fishing boats. He ran out expecting to see bloodshed. Instead, he saw the rival groups throwing each other down into the mudflats and laughing with glee. This was their way of resolving their differences. The incoming tidal waters then washed away their grievances—but not before they dragged Fr. Cole into the mud with them.

Egalitarianism

As Americans, Maryknollers also hold that all men and women are created equal. Even as the country struggles with the notion of gender equality, the Maryknoll Society finds itself in a double bind. How does an American function in a Church that is anything but egalitarian, especially in regard to women in positions of decision making and power? On the other hand, how does a Catholic function in a

country that does not respect life in all its stages? Perhaps nothing exacerbates tension between Maryknollers as Americans and Maryknollers as Catholics more than the various liberation movements. Patriarchy, male supremacy, and conversely, the suppression of women's rights and roles has become repugnant for many, but by no means all, Maryknollers. This often puts them increasingly on a collision course with some official Church policies. But Maryknollers who find themselves in solidarity with women or other oppressed minorities do so not simply out of an American sense of justice and fairness but more importantly from their belief that such solidarity flows directly from gospel imperatives. Just as it took the United States more than 150 years to realize that its notion of equality applied to all races and genders, so, too, the reign of God as proclaimed by Christ remains a work in progress within the Church.

Fr. Dick Baker has a heart-to-heart talk with a man in Ethiopia.

"There is much more I have to tell you,
but you could not bear it now."
—John 16:12

Onward

As the Catholic Foreign Mission Society of America, Maryknollers strive to promote the best of what it means to be both Catholic and American as a society of men ministering overseas. It not only acts as a bridge between different cultures, it also cross-fertilizes the United States with gospel values and the Roman Catholic Church with democratic ideals. Being the foreign mission society of the Church in the United States, Maryknoll is uniquely positioned to show the better side of America to the people of the world and introduce the good people of the world to their brothers and sisters in America.

The men of Maryknoll are a symphony of diverse and sometimes contradictory forces. When the best of Catholicism

Fr. Sean Burke shares a laugh with an elderly Chinese woman.

unites with the best of what it means to be an American, Maryknollers become dynamic witnesses to the reign of God. At other times, they may bring democratic ideals to the institutional church. Or they may challenge the policies and practices of the United States with gospel values, especially concerning the poor.

As Maryknollers struggle as a Society with fewer and older members, physical limitations and diminishment, the natural tendency is to circle the wagons or shut down altogether. For men who identified with doing and who discovered self-worth in being active, especially overseas, the prospect of old age and debilitating illness are particularly daunting. On another level, this phase of Maryknoll's life may be exactly what the larger American society needs to see and witness, and more important, it may be exactly where God wants it to be.

In a culture that all but idolizes youth and beauty and puts a high premium on productivity, old age seems a curse. Making the transition from young and active to aged and passive is no easier for Maryknollers than for people on the outside. Yet there is truth to be discovered in limitations and grace to be experienced in diminishment. Many Maryknollers spent their lives in cultures that venerated the elderly. No wonder many are reluctant to retire in the States where the aged are all but invisible and the disabled viewed as a liability. Perhaps older Maryknollers have one final mission to serve and one final example to offer: to bear witness to people in the United States that the elderly are a treasury of experiences and wisdom. In old age and infirmities, Maryknollers can show how, like St. Paul, to make up in their flesh what is lacking from the sufferings of Christ (1 Colossians 24).

The spirit and spiritualities of the Maryknoll Fathers and Brothers transcend race, gender, age, class, and ethnicity to create a bond with all peoples, with the planet, with one another, and with God. In this they are truly catholic, that is, universal. The spirit of Maryknoll radiates through these myriad relationships to reflect the light of Christ in a unique and compelling way. Under the guidance of Our Lady of Maryknoll, the Catholic Foreign Mission Society of America will continue as long as there are two or more Catholics in the United States willing to gather in Jesus' name to cross borders and go to the ends of the earth for the sake of the reign of God.